The Philosophy of EXISTENTIALISM

by Gabriel Marcel

THE PHILOSOPHY OF

existentialism

the citadel press • secaucus, n.j.

The last piece in this volume, *An Essay in Autobiography,* is taken from the commemorative book on M. Marcel's work written by a group of French thinkers and critics and edited by Etienne Gilson, *Existentialisme Chrétien* (Collection "Présences," Plon, Paris, 1947).

Translated by
MANYA HARARI

Copyright© 1956 by Philosophical Library
All rights reserved
Published by Citadel Press
A division of Lyle Stuart Inc.
120 Enterprise Ave., Secaucus, N.J. 07094
In Canada: General Publishing Co. Limited
Don Mills, Ontario
Manufactured in the United States of America

ISBN 0-8065-0901-5

INTRODUCTION

Of the three papers which form the main part of this book, the first, written in 1933, explains the main lines of my position, which have not changed since that time. The second, written in Paris in January, 1946, is a critical survey of the philosophy of Jean-Paul Sartre. The third, written in February, 1946, seeks to define the "existentialist" doctrine which I personally hold, while making certain reservations in regard to a vocabulary which has become fashionable but which is, in many ways, open to criticism.

Thus the reader is offered a kind of diptych showing the two aspects of the contemporary existentialist school in France, aspects which are, in the main, opposed to one another, though they are in some respects complementary.

I believe that it is in my essay entitled *Existence et Objectivité*, published in the *Revue de Métaphysique et de Morale* in 1925 that the main lines of this new development were first formulated in France. I had not then read Kierkegaard, who was still almost unknown in France nor had Heidegger or Jaspers as yet published their main works. As against this, my essay, *On the Ontological Mystery*, was written shortly after I had read Jaspers' *Système de Philos-*

ophie, though I cannot tell how far this work favoured the development of its principal themes. Not only my terminology but my whole spiritual and religious orientation are quite different from those of Jaspers. Nevertheless, I feel obscurely that I owe a real debt to this noble and profound thinker, and I am anxious to acknowledge the inward and almost indefinable influence which he has exercised over my own mind.

GABRIEL MARCEL

CONTENTS

Introduction 5

On the Ontological Mystery 9

Existence and Human Freedom 47

Testimony and Existentialism 91

An Essay in Autobiography 104

ON THE ONTOLOGICAL MYSTERY

The title of this essay is likely to annoy the philosopher as much as to startle the layman, since philosophers are inclined to leave mystery either to the theologians or else to the vulgarisers, whether of mysticism or of occultism, such as Maeterlinck. Moreover, the term *ontological*, which has only the vaguest meaning for the layman, has become discredited in the eyes of Idealist philosophers; while the term *mystery* is reserved by those thinkers who are imbued with the ideas of Scholasticism for the revealed mysteries of religion.

Thus my terminology is clearly open to criticism from all sides. But I can find no other which is adequate to the body of ideas which I intend to put forward and on which my whole outlook is based. Readers of my *Journal Métaphysique* will see that they represent the term of the whole spiritual and philosophical evolution which I have described in that book.

Rather than to begin with abstract definitions and dialectical arguments which may be discouraging at the outset, I should like to start with a sort of global and intuitive characterisation of the man in whom the sense of the ontological—the sense of being—is lacking, or, to speak more correctly, of the man who has lost the awareness of this sense. Generally speaking, modern man is in this condition; if ontological demands worry him at all, it is only dully, as an obscure impulse. Indeed I wonder if a psychoanalytical method, deeper and more discerning than any that has been evolved until now, would not reveal the morbid effects of the repression of this sense and of the ignoring of this need.

The characteristic feature of our age seems to me to be what might be called the misplacement of the idea of function, taking function in its current sense which includes both the vital and the social functions.

The individual tends to appear both to himself and to others as an agglomeration of functions. As a result of deep historical causes, which can as yet be understood only in part, he has been led to see himself more and more as a mere assemblage of functions, the hierarchical interrelation of which seems to him questionable or at least subject to conflicting interpretations.

To take the vital functions first. It is hardly necessary to point out the role which historical materialism on the one hand, and Freudian doctrines on the other, have played in restricting the concept of man.

Then there are the social functions—those of the consumer, the producer, the citizen, etc.

Between these two there is, in theory, room for the psychological functions as well; but it is easy to see how these will tend to be interpreted in relation either to the social or the vital functions, so that their independence will be threatened and their specific character put in doubt. In this sense, Comte, served by his total incomprehension of psychical reality, displayed an almost prophetic instinct when he excluded psychology from his classification of sciences.

So far we are still dealing only with abstractions, but

nothing is easier than to find concrete illustrations in this field.

Travelling on the Underground, I often wonder with a kind of dread what can be the inward reality of the life of this or that man employed on the railway—the man who opens the doors, for instance, or the one who punches the tickets. Surely everything both within him and outside him conspires to identify this man with his functions—meaning not only with his functions as worker, as trade union member or as voter, but with his vital functions as well. The rather horrible expression "time table" perfectly describes his life. So many hours for each function. Sleep too is a function which must be discharged so that the other functions may be exercised in their turn. The same with pleasure, with relaxation; it is logical that the weekly allowance of recreation should be determined by an expert on hygiene; recreation is a psycho-organic function which must not be neglected any more than, for instance, the function of sex. We need go no further; this sketch is sufficient to suggest the emergence of a kind of vital schedule; the details will vary with the country, the climate, the profession, etc., but what matters is that there is a schedule.

It is true that certain disorderly elements—sickness, accidents of every sort—will break in on the smooth working of the system. It is therefore natural that the individual should be overhauled at regular intervals like a watch (this is often done in America). The hospital plays the part of the inspection bench or the repair shop. And it is from this same standpoint of function that such essential problems as birth control will be examined.

As for death, it becomes, objectively and functionally, the

scrapping of what has ceased to be of use and must be written off as total loss.

I need hardly insist on the stifling impression of sadness produced by this functionalised world. It is sufficient to recall the dreary image of the retired official, or those urban Sundays when the passers-by look like people who have retired from life. In such a world, there is something mocking and sinister even in the tolerance awarded to the man who has retired from his work.

But besides the sadness felt by the onlooker, there is the dull, intolerable unease of the actor himself who is reduced to living as though he were in fact submerged by his functions. This uneasiness is enough to show that there is in all this some appalling mistake, some ghastly misinterpretation, implanted in defenceless minds by an increasingly inhuman social order and an equally inhuman philosophy (for if the philosophy has prepared the way for the order, the order has also shaped the philosophy).

I have written on another occasion that, provided it is taken in its metaphysical and not its physical sense, the distinction between the *full* and the *empty* seems to me more fundamental than that between the *one* and the *many*. This is particularly applicable to the case in point. Life in a world centered on function is liable to despair because in reality this world is *empty*, it rings hollow; and if it resists this temptation it is only to the extent that there come into play from within it and in its favour certain hidden forces which are beyond its power to conceive or to recognise.

It should be noted that this world is, on the one hand, riddled with problems and, on the other, determined to allow no room for mystery. I shall come back to this distinction between problem and mystery which I believe to be fundamental. For the moment I shall only point out that to eliminate or to try to eliminate mystery is (in this functionalist world) to bring into play in the face of events which break in on the course of existence—such as birth, love and death—that psychological and pseudo-scientific category of the "purely natural" which deserves a study to itself. In reality, this is nothing more than the remains of a degraded rationalism from whose standpoint cause explains effect and accounts for it exhaustively. There exists in such a world, nevertheless, an infinity of problems, since the causes are not known to us in detail and thus leave room for unlimited research. And in addition to these theoretical puzzles there are innumerable technical problems, bound up with the difficulty of knowing how the various functions, once they have been inventoried and labelled, can be made to work together without doing one another harm. These theoretical and technical questions are interdependent, for the theoretical problems arise out of the different techniques while the technical problems can not be solved without a measure of pre-established theoretical knowledge.

In such a world the ontological need, the need of being, is exhausted in exact proportion to the breaking up of personality on the one hand and, on the other, to the triumph of the category of the "purely natural" and the consequent atrophy of the faculty of *wonder*.

But to come at last to the ontological need itself; can we not approach it directly and attempt to define it? In reality this can only be done to a limited extent. For reasons which I shall develop later, I suspect that the characteristic of this need is that it can never be wholly clear to itself.

To try to describe it without distorting it we shall have to say something like this:

Being is—or should be—necessary. It is impossible that everything should be reduced to a play of successive appearances which are inconsistent with each other ("inconsistent" is essential), or, in the words of Shakespeare, to "a tale told by an idiot." I aspire to participate in this being, in this reality—and perhaps this aspiration is already a degree of participation, however rudimentary.

Such a need, it may be noted, is to be found at the heart of the most inveterate pessimism. Pessimism has no meaning unless it signifies: it would surely be well if there were being, but there is no being, and I, who observe this fact, am therefore nothing.

As for defining the word "being," let us admit that it is extremely difficult. I would merely suggest this method of approach: being is what withstands—or what would withstand—an exhaustive analysis bearing on the data of experience and aiming to reduce them step by step to elements increasingly devoid of intrinsic or significant value. (An analysis of this kind is attempted in the theoretical works of Freud.)

When the pessimist Besme says in *La Ville* that *nothing is,* he means precisely this, that there is no experience that withstands this analytical test. And it is always towards death regarded as the manifestation, the proof of this ultimate nothingness that the kind of inverted apologetic which arises out of absolute pessimism will inevitably gravitate.

A philosophy which refuses to endorse the ontological need is, nevertheless, possible; indeed, generally speaking, contemporary thought tends towards this abstention. But at this point a distinction must be made between two different attitudes which are sometimes confused: one which consists in a systematic reserve (it is that of agnosticism in all its forms), and the other, bolder and more coherent, which regards the ontological need as the expression of an outworn body of dogma liquidated once and for all by the Idealist critique.

The former appears to me to be purely negative: it is merely the expression of an intellectual policy of "not raising the question."

The latter, on the contrary, claims to be based on a positive theory of thought. This is not the place for a detailed critical study of this philosophy. I shall only note that it seems to me to tend towards an unconscious relativism, or else towards a monism which ignores the personal in all its form, ignores the tragic and denies the transcendent, seeking to reduce it to its caricatural expressions which distort its essential character. I shall also point out that, just because this philosophy continually stresses the activity of verification, it ends by ignoring *presence*—that inward realisation of presence through love which infinitely transcends all possible verification because it exists in an immediacy beyond all conceivable mediation. This will be clearer to some extent from what follows.

Thus I believe for my part that the ontological need cannot be silenced by an arbitrary dictatorial act which mutilates the life of the spirit at its roots. It remains true, nevertheless, that such an act is possible, and the conditions of our life are such that we can well believe that we are carrying it out; this must never be forgotten.

These preliminary reflections on the ontological need are sufficient to bring out its indeterminate character and to reveal a fundamental paradox. To formulate this need is to raise a host of questions: Is there such a thing as being? What is it? etc. Yet immediately an abyss opens under my feet: I who ask these questions about being, how can I be sure that I exist?

Yet surely I, who formulate this *problem*, should be able to remain *outside* it—*before* or *beyond* it? Clearly this is not so. The more I consider it the more I find that this problem tends inevitably to invade the proscenium from which it is excluded in theory: it is only by means of a fiction that Idealism in its traditional form seeks to maintain on the margin of being the consciousness which asserts it or denies it.

So I am inevitably forced to ask: Who am I—I who question being? How am I qualified to begin this investigation? If I do not exist, how can I succeed in it? And if I do exist, how can I be sure of this fact?

Contrary to the opinion which suggests itself at this point, I believe that on this plane the *cogito* cannot help us at all. Whatever Descartes may have thought of it himself, the only certainty with which it provides us concerns only the epistemological subject as organ of objective cognition. As I have written elsewhere, the *cogito* merely guards the threshold of objective validity, and that is strictly all; this is proved by the indeterminate character of the *I*. The *I am* is, to my mind, a global statement which it is impossible to break down into its component parts.

There remains a possible objection; it might be said: Either the being designated in the question "What am I?" concerns the subject of cognition, and in this case we are on the plane of the *cogito*; or else that which you call the ontological need is merely the extreme point (or perhaps only the fallacious transposition) of a need which is, in reality, vital and with which the metaphysician is not concerned.

But is it not a mistake arbitrarily to divide the question, *Who am I?* from the ontological "problem" taken as a whole? The truth is that neither of the two can be dealt with separately, but that when they are taken together, they cancel one another out *as problems.*

It should be added that the Cartesian position is inseparable from a form of dualism which I, for my part, would unhesitatingly reject. To raise the ontological problem is to raise the question of being as a whole and of oneself seen as a totality.

But should we not ask ourselves if we must not reject this dissociation between the intellectual and the vital, with its resultant over- or under-estimation of the one or the other? Doubtless it is legitimate to establish certain distinctions within the unity of the being who thinks and who endeavours to *think himself;* but it is only beyond such distinctions that the ontological problem can arise and it must relate to that being seen in his all-comprehensive unity.

To sum up our reflections at this point, we find that we are dealing with an urge towards an affirmation—yet an affirmation which it seems impossible to make, since it is not until it has been made that I can regard myself as qualified to make it.

It should be noted that this difficulty never arises at a time when I am actually faced with a problem to be solved. In such a case I work on the data, but everything leads me to believe that I need not take into account the *I* who is at work—it is a factor which is presupposed and nothing more.

Here, on the contrary, which I would call the ontological status of the investigator assumes a decisive importance. Yet so long as I am concerned with thought itself I seem to follow an endless regression. But by the very fact of recognising it as endless I transcend it in a certain way: I see that this process takes place within an affirmation of being—an affirmation which I *am* rather than an affirmation which I *utter*: by uttering it I break it, I divide it, I am on the point of betraying it.

It might be said, by way of an approximation, that my inquiry into being presupposes an affirmation in regard to which I am, in a sense, passive, *and of which I am the stage rather than the subject*. But this is only at the extreme limit of thought, a limit which I cannot reach without falling into contradiction. I am therefore led to assume or to recognise a form of participation which has the reality of a subject; this participation cannot be, by definition, an *object* of thought; it cannot serve as a solution—it appears beyond the realm of problems: it is meta-problematical.

Conversely, it will be seen that, if the meta-problematical can be asserted at all, it must be conceived as transcending the opposition between the subject who asserts the existence of being, on the one hand, and being *as asserted by that subject*, on the other, and as underlying it in a given sense. To postulate the meta-problematical is to postulate the primacy of being over knowledge (not of being as *asserted*, but of being as *asserting itself*); it is to recognise that knowledge is, as it were, environed by being, that it is interior to it in a certain sense—a sense perhaps analogous to that which Paul Claudel tried to define in his *Art Poètique*. From this standpoint, contrary to what epistemology seeks vainly to establish, there exists well and truly a mystery of cognition; knowledge is contingent on a participation in being for which no epistemology can account because it continually presupposes it.

At this point we can begin to define the distinction between mystery and problem. A mystery is a problem which encroaches upon its own data, invading them, as it were, and thereby transcending itself as a simple problem. A set of examples will help us to grasp the content of this definition.

It is evident that there exists a mystery of the union of the body and the soul. The indivisible unity always inadequately expressed by such phrases as I *have a body,* I *make use of my body,* I *feel my body,* etc., can be neither analysed nor reconstituted out of precedent elements. It is not only data, I would say that it is the basis of data, in the sense of being my own presence to myself, a presence of which the act of self-consciousness is, in the last analysis, only an inadequate symbol.

It will be seen at once that there is no hope of establishing an exact frontier between problem and mystery. For in reflecting on a mystery we tend inevitably to degrade it to the level of a problem. This is particularly clear in the case of the problem of evil.

In reflecting upon evil, I tend, almost inevitably, to regard it as a disorder which I view from outside and of which I seek to discover the causes or the secret aims. Why is it that the "mechanism" functions so defectively? Or is the defect merely apparent and due to a real defect of my vision? In this case the defect is in myself, yet it remains objective in relation to my thought, which discovers it and observes it. But evil which is only stated or observed is no longer evil which is suffered: in fact, it ceases to be evil. In reality, I can only grasp it as evil in the measure in which it *touches* me—that is to say, in the measure in which I am *involved,* as one is involved in a law-suit. Being "involved" is the fundamental fact; I cannot leave it out of account except by an unjustifiable fiction, for in doing so, I proceed as though I were God, and a God who is an onlooker at that.

This brings out how the distinction between what is *in me* and what is only *before me* can break down. This distinction falls under the blow of a certain kind of thought: thought at one remove.

But it is, of course, in love that the obliteration of this frontier can best be seen. It might perhaps even be shown that the domain of the meta-problematical coincides with that of love, and that love is the only starting point for the understanding of such mysteries as that of body and soul, which, in some manner, is its expression.

Actually, it is inevitable that, in being brought to bear on love, thought which has not thought itself—unreflected reflection—should tend to dissolve its meta-problematical character and interpret it in terms of abstract concepts, such as the will to live, the will to power, the *libido*, etc. On the other hand, since the domain of the problematical is that of the objectively valid, it will be extremely difficult—if not impossible—to refute these interpretations without changing to a new ground: a ground on which, to tell the truth, they lose their meaning. Yet I have the assurance, the certainty—and it envelops me like a protective cloak—that for as much as I really love I must not be concerned with these attempts at devaluation.

It will be asked: What is the criterion of true love? It must be answered that there is no criteriology except in the order of the objective and the problematical; but we can already see at a distance the eminent ontological value to be assigned to fidelity.

Let us take another illustration, more immediate and more

particular, which may shed some light on the distinction between problem and mystery.

Say that I have made an encounter which has left a deep and lasting trace on all my life. It may happen to anyone to experience the deep spiritual significance of such a meeting—yet this is something which philosophers have commonly ignored or disdained, doubtless because it effects only the particular person as person—it cannot be universalised, it does not concern rational being in general.

It is clear that such a meeting raises, if you will, a problem; but it is equally clear that the solution of this problem will always fall short of the only question that matters. Suppose that I am told, for instance: "The reason you have met this person in this place is that you both like the same kind of scenery, or that you both need the same kind of treatment for your health"—the explanation means nothing. Crowds of people who apparently share my tastes were in the Engadine or in Florence at the time I was there; and there are always numbers of patients suffering from the same disease as myself at the health resort I frequent. But neither this supposed identity of tastes nor this common affliction has brought us together in any real sense; it has nothing to do with that intimate and unique affinity with which we are dealing. At the same time, it would be transgression of this valid reasoning to treat this affinity as if it were itself the cause and to say: "It is precisely this which has determined our meeting."

Hence I am in the presence of a mystery. That is to say, of a reality rooted in what is beyond the domain of the problematical properly so called. Shall we avoid the difficulty by saying that it was after all nothing but a coincidence, a lucky chance? But the whole of me immediately protests against this empty formula, this vain negation of what I apprehend with the deepest of my being. Once again we are brought back to our first definition of a mystery as a problem which encroaches upon its own data: I who inquire into the meaning and the possibility of this meeting, I cannot place myself outside it or before it; I am engaged in this encounter, I depend upon it, I am inside it in a certain sense, it envelops me and it comprehends me—even if it is not comprehended by me. Thus it is only by a kind of betrayal or denial that I can say: "After all, it might not have happened, I would still have been what I was, and what I am to-day." Nor must it be said: I have been changed by it as by an outward cause. No, it has developed me from within, it has acted in me as an inward principle.

But this is very difficult to grasp without distortion. I shall be inevitably tempted to react against this sense of the inwardness of the encounter, tempted by my probity itself, by what from a certain standpoint I must judge to be the best—or at least the safest—of myself.

There is a danger that these explanations may strengthen in the minds of my readers a preliminary objection which must be stated at once.

It will be said: The meta-problematical of which you speak is after all a content of thought; how then should we not ask ourselves what is its mode of existence? What assures us of its existence at all? Is it not itself problematical in the highest degree?

My answer is categorical: To think, or, rather, to assert, the meta-problematical is to assert it as indubitably real, as a thing of which I cannot doubt without falling into contradiction. We are in a sphere where it is no longer possible to dissociate the idea itself from the certainty or the degree of certainty which pertains to it. Because this idea *is* certainty, it *is* the assurance of itself; it is, in this sense, something other and something more than an idea. As for the term *content of thought* which figured in the objection, it is deceptive in the highest degree. For content is, when all is said and done, derived from experience; whereas it is only by a way of liberation and detachment from experience that we can possibly rise to the level of the meta-problematical and of mystery. This liberation must be *real*; this detachment must be *real*; they must not be an abstraction, that is to say a fiction recognised as such.

And this at last brings us to recollection, for it is in recollection and in this alone that this detachment is accomplished. I am convinced, for my part, that no ontology—that is to say, no apprehension of ontological mystery in whatever degree—is possible except to a being who is capable of recollecting himself, and of thus proving that he is not a living creature pure and simple, a creature, that is to say, which is at the mercy of its life and without a hold upon it.

It should be noted that recollection, which has received little enough attention from pure philosophers, is very difficult to define—if only because it transcends the dualism of being and action or, more correctly, because it reconciles in itself these two aspects of the antinomy. The word means what it says—the act whereby I re-collect myself as a unity; but this hold, this grasp upon myself, is also relaxation and abandon. *Abandon to . . . relaxation in the presence of* . . . —yet there is no noun for these prepositions to govern. The way stops at the threshold.

Here, as in every other sphere, problems will be raised, and it is the psychologist who will raise them. All that must be noted is that the psychologist is no more in a position to shed light on the metaphysical bearing of recollection than on the noetic value of knowledge.

It is within recollection that I take up my position—or, rather, I become capable of taking up my position—in regard to my life; I withdraw from it in a certain way, but not as the pure subject of cognition; *in this withdrawal I carry with me that which I am and which perhaps my life is not.* This brings out the gap between my being and my life. I am not my life; and if I can judge my life—a fact I cannot deny without falling into a radical scepticism which is nothing other than despair—it is only on condition that I encounter myself within recollection beyond all possible judgment and, I would add, beyond all representation. Recollection is doubtless what is least spectacular in the soul; it does not consist in looking at something, it is an inward hold, an inward reflection, and it might be asked in passing whether it should not be seen as the ontological basis of memory— that principle of effective and non-representational unity on which the possibility of remembrance rests. The double meaning of "recollection" in English is revealing.

It may be asked: is not recollection identical with that dialectical moment of the turning to oneself (*retour sur soi*) or else with the *fuer sich sein* which is the central theme of German Idealism?

I do not think so. To withdraw into oneself is not to be for oneself nor to mirror oneself in the intelligible unity of subject and object. On the contrary. I would say that here we come up against the paradox of that actual mystery whereby the I into which I withdraw ceases, for as much, to belong to itself. "You are not your own"—this great saying of St. Paul assumes in this connection its full concrete and ontological significance; it is the nearest approach to the reality for which we are groping. It will be asked: is not this reality an object of intuition? Is not that which you term "recollection" the same as what others have termed "intuition"?

But this again seems to me to call for the utmost prudence. If intuition can be mentioned in this content at all, it is not an intuition which is, or can be, given as such.

The more an intuition is central and basic in the being whom it illuminates, the less it is capable of turning back and apprehending itself.

Moreover, if we reflect on what an intuitive knowledge of being could possibly be, we see that it could never figure in a collection, a procession of simple experiences or *Erlebnisse*, which all have this characteristic that they can be at times absorbed and at others isolated and, as it were, uncovered. Hence, any effort to remember such an intuition, to represent it to oneself, is inevitably fruitless. From this point of view, to be told of an intuitive knowledge of being is like being invited to play on a soundless piano. Such an intuition cannot be brought out into the light of day, for the simple reason that we do not possess it.

We are here at the most difficult point of our whole discussion. Rather than to speak of intuition in this context, we should say that we are dealing with an assurance which underlies the entire development of thought, even of discursive thought; it can therefore be approached only by a second reflection—a reflection whereby I ask myself how and from what starting point I was able to proceed in my initial reflection, which itself postulated the ontological, but without knowing it. This second reflection is recollection in the measure in which recollection can be self-conscious.

It is indeed annoying to have to use such abstract language in a matter which is not one of dialectics *ad usum philosophorum*, but of what is the most vital and, I would add, the most dramatic moment in the rhythm of consciousness seeking to be conscious of itself.

It is this dramatic aspect which must now be brought out.

Let us recall what we said earlier on: that the ontological need, the need of being, can deny itself. In a different context we said that being and life do not coincide; my life, and by reflection all life, may appear to me as for ever inadequate to something which I carry within me, which in a sense I am, but which reality rejects and excludes. Despair is possible in any form, at any moment and to any degree, and this betrayal may seem to be counselled, if not forced upon us, by the very structure of the world we live in. The deathly aspect of this world may, from a given standpoint, be regarded as a ceaseless incitement to denial and to suicide. It could even be said in this sense that the fact that suicide is always possible is the essential starting point of any genuine metaphysical thought.

It may be surprising to find in the course of this calm and abstract reasoning such verbal star turns—words so emotionally charged—as "suicide" and "betrayal." They are not a concession to sensationalism. I am convinced that it is in drama and through drama that metaphysical thought grasps and defines itself *in concreto*. Two years ago, in a lecture on the "Problem of Christian Philosophy" which he delivered at Louvain, M. Jacques Maritain said: "There is nothing easier for a philosophy than to become tragic, it has only to let itself go to its human weight." The allusion was doubtless to the speculation of a Heidegger. I believe, on the contrary, that the natural trend of philosophy leads it into a sphere where it seems that tragedy has simply vanished—evaporated at the touch of abstract thought. This is borne out by the work of many contemporary Idealists. Because they ignore the person, offering it up to I know not what ideal truth, to what principle of pure inwardness, they are unable to grasp those tragic factors of human existence to which I have alluded above; they banish them, together with illness and everything akin to it, to I know not what disreputable suburb of thought outside the ken of any philosopher worthy of the name. But, as I have stressed earlier on, this attitude is intimately bound up with the rejection of the ontological need; indeed, it is the same thing.

If I have stressed despair, betrayal and suicide, it is because these are the most manifest expressions of the will to negation as applied to being.

Let us take despair. I have in mind the act by which one despairs of reality as a whole, as one might despair of a person. This appears to be the result, or the immediate translation into other terms, of a kind of balance sheet. Inasmuch as I am able to evaluate the world of reality (and, when all is said and done, what I am unable to evaluate is for me as if it were not) I can find nothing in it that withstands that process of dissolution at the heart of things which I have discovered and traced. I believe that at the root of despair there is always this affirmation: "There is nothing in the realm of reality to which I can give credit—no security, no guarantee." It is a statement of complete insolvency.

As against this, hope is what implies credit. Contrary to what was thought by Spinoza, who seems to me to have confused two quite distinct notions, fear is correlated to desire and not to hope, whereas what is negatively correlated to hope is the act which consists in putting things at their worst—an act which is strikingly illustrated by what is known as defeatism, and which is ever in danger of being degraded into the desire of the worst. Hope consists in asserting that there is at the heart of being, beyond all data, beyond all inventories and all calculations, a mysterious principle which is in connivance with me, which cannot but will that which I will, if what I will deserves to be willed and is, in fact, willed by the whole of my being.

We have now come to the centre of what I have called the ontological mystery, and the simplest illustrations will be the best. To hope against all hope that a person whom I love will recover from a disease which is said to be incurable is to say: It is impossible that I should be alone in willing this cure; it is impossible that reality in its inward depth should be hostile or so much as indifferent to what I assert is in itself a good. It is quite useless to tell me of discouraging *cases* or *examples*: beyond all experience, all probability, all statistics, I assert that a given order shall be re-established, that reality *is* on my side in willing it to be so. I do not wish: I assert; such is the prophetic tone of true hope.

No doubt I shall be told: "In the immense majority of cases this is an illusion." But it is of the essence of hope to exclude the consideration of cases; moreover, it can be shown that there exists an ascending dialectic of hope, whereby hope rises to a plane which transcends the level of all possible empirical disproof—the plane of salvation as opposed to that of success in whatever form.

It remains true, nevertheless, that the correlation of hope and despair subsists until the end; they seem to me inseparable. I mean that while the structure of the world we live in permits—and may even seem to counsel—absolute despair, yet it is only such a world that can give rise to an unconquerable hope. If only for this reason, we cannot be sufficiently thankful to the great pessimists in the history of thought; they have carried through an inward experience which needed to be made and of which the radical possibility no apologetics should disguise; they have prepared our minds to understand that despair can be what it was for Nietzsche (though on an infra-ontological level and in a domain fraught with mortal dangers) the springboard to the loftiest affirmation.

At the same time, it remains certain that, for as much as hope is a mystery, its mystery can be ignored or converted into a problem. Hope is then regarded as a desire which wraps itself up in illusory judgments to distort an objective reality which it is interested in disguising from itself. What happens in this case is what we have already observed in connection with encounter and with love; it is because mystery can—and, in a sense, logically must—be degraded into a problem that an interpretation such as that of Spinoza, with all the confusion it implies, had to be put forward sooner or later. It is important and must be stressed that this attitude has nothing against it so long as our standpoint is on the hither-side of the realm of the ontological. Just as long as my attitude towards reality is that of someone who is not involved in it, but who judges it his duty to draw up its minutes as exactly as possible (and this is by definition the attitude of the scientist), I am justified in maintaining in regard to it a sort of principle of mistrust, which in theory is unlimited in its application; such is the legitimate standpoint of the workman in the laboratory, who must in no way prejudge the result of his analysis, and who can all the better envisage *the worst*, because at this level the very notion of worst is empty of meaning. But an investigation of this sort, which is just like that of an accountant going through the books, takes place on the hither-side of the order of mystery, an order in which the problem encroaches upon its own data.

It would indeed be a profound illusion to believe that I can still maintain this same attitude when I undertake an inquiry, say, into the value of life; it would be a paralogism to suppose that I can pursue such an inquiry as though my own life were not at issue.

Hence, between hope—the reality of hope in the heart of the one whom it inhabits—and the judgment brought to bear upon it by a mind chained to objectivity there exists the same barrier as that which separates a pure mystery from a pure problem.

This brings us to a nodal point of our subject, where certain intimate connections can be traced.

The world of the problematical is the world of fear and desire, which are inseparable; at the same time, it is that world of the functional—or of what can be fuctionalised—which was defined at the beginning of this essay; finally, it is the kingdom of technics of whatever sort. Every technique serves, or can be made to serve, some desire or some fear; conversely, every desire as every fear tends to invent its appropriate technique. From this standpoint, despair consists in the recognition of the ultimate inefficacy of all technics, joined to the inability or the refusal to change over to a new ground—a ground where all technics are seen to be incompatible with the fundamental nature of being, which itself escapes our grasp (in so far as our grasp is limited to the world of objects and to this alone). It is for this reason that we seem nowadays to have entered upon the very era of despair; we have not ceased to believe in technics, that is to envisage reality as a complex of problems; yet at the same time the failure of technics *as a whole* is as discernible to us as its *partial* triumphs. To the question: what can man achieve? we continue to reply: He can achieve as much as his technics; yet we are obliged to admit that these technics are unable *to save man himself,* and even that they are apt to conclude the most sinister alliance with the enemy he bears within him.

I have said that man is *at the mercy of his technics.* This must be understood to mean that he is increasingly incapable of controlling his technics, or rather of *controlling his own control.* This control of his own control, which is nothing else than the expression on the plane of active life of what I have called thought at one remove, cannot find its centre or its support anywhere except in recollection.

It will be objected that even those whose faith in technics is strongest are bound to admit that there exist enormous realms which are outside man's control. But what matters is the spirit in which this admission is made. We have to recognise that we have no control over meteorological conditions, but the question is: do we consider it desirable and just that we should have such control? The more the sense of the ontological tends to disappear, the more unlimited become the claims of the mind which has lost it to a kind of cosmic governance, because it is less and less capable of examining its own credentials to the exercise of such dominion.

It must be added that the more the disproportion grows between the claims of the technical intelligence on the one hand, and the persisting fragility and precariousness of what remains its material substratum on the other, the more acute becomes the constant danger of despair which threatens this intelligence. From this standpoint there is truly an intimate dialectical correlation between the optimism of technical progress and the philosophy of despair which seems inevitably to emerge from it—it is needless to insist on the examples offered by the world of to-day.

It will perhaps be said: This optimism of technical progress is animated by great hope. How is hope in this sense to be reconciled with the ontological interpretation of hope?

I believe it must be answered that, *speaking metaphysically, the only genuine hope is hope in what does not depend on ourselves,* hope springing from humility and not from pride. This brings us to the consideration of another aspect of the mystery—a mystery which, in the last analysis, is one and unique—on which I am endeavouring to throw some light.

The metaphysical problem of pride—*hubris*—which was perceived by the Greeks and which has been one of the essential themes of Christian theology, seems to me to have been almost completely ignored by modern philosophers other than theologians. It has become a domain reserved for the moralist. Yet from my own standpoint it is an essential—if not the vital—question. It is sufficient to recall Spinoza's definition of *superbia* in his *Ethics* (III, def. XXVIII) to see how far he was from grasping the problem: "Pride is an exaggeratedly good opinion of ourselves which arises from self-love." In reality, this is a definition of vanity. As for pride, it consists in drawing one's strength solely from oneself. The proud man is cut off from a certain form of communion with his fellow men, which pride, acting as a principle of destruction, tends to break down. Indeed, this destructiveness can be equally well directed against the self; pride is in no way incompatible with self-hate; this is what Spinoza does not seem to have perceived.

An important objection may be raised at the point we have now reached.

It will perhaps be said: Is not that which you are justifying ontologically in reality a kind of moral quietism which is satisfied by passive acceptance, resignation and inert hope? But what, then, becomes of man as man, as active being? Are we to condemn action itself inasmuch as it implies a self-confidence which is akin to pride? Can it be that action itself is a kind of degradation?

This objection implies a series of misunderstandings.

To begin with, the idea of inert hope seems to me a contradiction in terms. Hope is not a kind of listless waiting; it underpins action or it runs before it, but it becomes degraded and lost once the action is spent. Hope seems to me, as it were, the prolongation into the unknown of an activity which is central—that is to say, rooted in being. Hence it has affinities, not with desire, but with the will. The will implies the same refusal to calculate possibilities, or at any rate it suspends this calculation. Could not hope therefore be defined as the will when it is made to bear on what does not depend on itself?

The experimental proof of this connection is that it is the most active saints who carry hope to its highest degree; this would be inconceivable if hope were simply an inactive state of the soul. The mistake so often made here comes from a stoical representation of the will as a stiffening of the soul, whereas it is on the contrary relaxation and creation.

The term "creation," which occurs here for the first time, is, nevertheless, decisive. Where there is creation there can be no degradation, and to the extent that technics are creative, or imply creativity, they are not degrading in any way. Degradation begins at the point where creativeness falls into self-imitation and self-hypnotism, stiffening and falling back on itself. This may, indeed, bring out the origin of the confusion which I denounced in the context of recollection.

Great is the temptation to confuse two distinct movements of the soul, whose opposition is blurred by the use of spacial metaphors. The stiffening, the contraction, the falling back on the self which are inseparable from pride, and which are indeed its symbol, must not be confused with the humble withdrawal which befits recollection and whereby I renew my contact with the ontological basis of my being.

There is every reason to think that such withdrawal in recollection is a presupposition of æsthetic creativity itself. Artistic creation, like scientific research, excludes the act of self-centring and self-hypnotism which is, ontologically speaking, pure negation.

It may perhaps seem that my thesis comes so near to that of Bergson as to coincide with it, but I do not think that this is the case. The terms almost invariably used by Bergson suggest that for him the essential character of creativity lay in its inventiveness, in its spontaneous innovation. But I wonder if by limiting our attention to this aspect of creation we do not lose sight of its ultimate significance, which is its deep-rootedness in being. It is at this point that I would bring in the notion of *creative fidelity*; it is a notion which is the more difficult to grasp and, above all, to define conceptually, because of its underlying and unfathomable paradox, and because it is at the very centre of the realm of the meta-problematical.

It is important to note that the idea of fidelity seems difficult to maintain in the context of Bergsonian metaphysics, because it will tend to be interpreted as a routine, as an observance in the pejorative sense of the word, as an arbitrary safeguard *against* the power of renewal which is the spirit itself.

I am inclined to think that there is something in this neglect of the values of fidelity which deeply vitiates the notion of static religion as it is put forward in *Les Deux Sources de la Morale et de la Religion*. It may perhaps be useful to devote some thought to creative fidelity in order to elucidate this point.

Faithfulness is, in reality, the exact opposite of inert conformism. It is the active recognition of something permanent, not formally, after the manner of a law, but ontologically; in this sense, it refers invariably to a presence, or to something which can be maintained within us and before us as a presence, but which, *ipso facto*, can be just as well ignored, forgotten and obliterated; and this reminds us of that menace of betrayal which, to my mind, overshadows our whole world.

It may perhaps be objected that we commonly speak of fidelity to a principle. But it remains to be seen if this is not an arbitrary transposition of the notion of fidelity. A principle, in so far as it is a mere abstract affirmation, can make no demands upon me because it owes the whole of its reality to the act whereby I sanction it or proclaim it. Fidelity to a principle as a principle is idolatry in the etymological sense of the word; it might be a sacred duty for me to deny a principle from which life has withdrawn and which I know that I no longer accept, for by continuing to conform my actions to it, it is myself—myself as presence—that I betray.

So little is fidelity akin to the inertia of conformism that it implies an active and continuous struggle against the forces of interior dissipation, as also against the sclerosis of habit. I may be told: This is nevertheless no more than a sort of active conservation which is the opposite of creation. We must, I think, go much further into the nature of fidelity and of presence before we can reply to this point.

If presence were merely an *idea* in us whose characteristic was that it was nothing more than itself, then indeed the most we could hope would be to maintain this idea in us or before us, as one keeps a photograph on a mantelpiece or in a cupboard. But it is of the nature of presence as presence to be uncircumscribed; and this takes us once again beyond the frontier of the problematical. Presence is mystery in the exact measure in which it is presence. Now fidelity is the active perpetuation of presence, the renewal of its benefits—of its virtue which consists in a mysterious incitement to create. Here again we may be helped by the consideration of æsthetic creativeness; for if artistic creation is conceivable, it can only be on condition that the world is present to the artist in a certain way—present to his heart and to his mind, present to his very being.

Thus if creative fidelity is conceivable, it is because fidelity is ontological in its principle, because it prolongs presence which itself corresponds to a certain kind of hold which being has upon us; because it multiplies and deepens the effect of this presence almost unfathomably in our lives. This seems to me to have almost inexhaustible consequences, if only for the relationships between the living and the dead.

I must insist once again: A presence to which we are faithful is not at all the same thing as the carefully preserved effigy of an object which has vanished; an effigy is, when all is said and done, nothing but a likeness; metaphysically it is *less* than the object, it is a diminution of the object. Whereas presence, on the contrary, is *more* than the object, it exceeds the object on every side. We are here at the opening of a vista at whose term death will appear as the *test of presence*. This is an essential point and we must consider it carefully.

It will no doubt be said: What a strange way of defining death! Death *is* a phenomenon definable in biological terms; it *is not* a test.

It must be answered: It is what it signifies and, moreover, what it signifies to a being who rises to the highest spiritual level to which it is possible for us to attain. It is evident that if I read in the newspaper of the death of Mr. So-and-so, who is for me nothing but a name, this event *is* for me nothing more than the subject of an announcement. But it is quite another thing in the case of a being who has been granted to me as a presence. In this case, everything depends on me, on my inward attitude of maintaining this presence which could be debased into an effigy.

It will be objected: This is nothing more than a description in recondite and unnecessarily metaphysical terms of a common psychological fact. It is evident that it depends upon us in a certain measure to enable the dead to survive in our memory, but this existence is no more than subjective.

I believe that the truth is altogether different and infinitely more mysterious. In saying, "It depends upon us that the dead should live on in our memory," we are still thinking of the idea in terms of a diminution or an effigy. We admit that the object has disappeared, but that there remains a likeness which it is in our power to keep, as a daily woman "keeps" a flat or a set of furniture. It is all too evident that this manner of keeping can have no ontological value whatsoever. But it is altogether different in the case where fidelity is creative in the sense which I have tried to define. A presence is a reality; it is a kind of influx; it depends upon us to be permeable to this influx, but not, to tell the truth, to call it forth. Creative fidelity consists in maintaining ourselves actively in a permeable state; and there is a mysterious interchange between this free act and the gift granted in response to it.

An objection which is the converse of the preceding one may be expected at this point. I will be told: "All right. You have now ceased to decorate a psychological platitude with metaphysical ornaments, but only to make a gratuitous assertion which is unproved and which is beyond all possible experimental proof; this was inevitable as soon as you replaced the ambiguous and neutral term 'presence' by the much more compromising term 'influx.'"

To reply to this objection, we must refer again to what I have already said of mystery and of recollection. Indeed, it is only on the meta-problematical level that the notion of influx can possibly be accepted. If it were taken in its objective sense, as an accretion of strength, we would indeed be faced with a thesis, not of metaphysics, but of physics, which would be open to every possible objection. When I say that a being is granted to me as a presence or as a being (it comes to the same, for he is not a being for me unless he is a presence), this means that I am unable to treat him as if he were merely placed in front of me; between him and me there arises a relationship which, in a sense, surpasses my awareness of him; he is not only before me, he is also within me—or, rather, these categories are transcended, they have no longer any meaning. The word influx conveys, though in a manner which is far too physical and spacial, the kind of interior accretion, of accretion from within, which comes into being as soon as presence is effective.

Great and almost invincible is the temptation to think that such effective presence can be only that of an object; but if we believed this we would fall back to the level of the problematical and remain on the hither-side of mystery; and against this belief fidelity raises up its voice: "Even if I cannot see you, if I cannot touch you, I feel that you are with me; it would be a denial of you not to be assured of this." *With* me: note the metaphysical value of this word, so rarely recognised by philosophers, which corresponds neither to a relationship of inherence or immanence nor to a relationship of exteriority. It is of the essence of genuine *coesse* —I must use the Latin word—that is to say, of genuine intimacy, to lend itself to the decomposition to which it is subjected by critical thought; but we already know that there exists another kind of thought, a thought which bears upon that thought itself, and is related to a bottled up yet efficacious underlying intuition, of which it suffers the attraction.

It must be added (and this brings us to the verge of another sphere) that the value of such intimacy, particularly in regard to the relation between the living and the dead, will be the higher and the more assured the more this intimacy is grounded in the realm of total spiritual availability (*disponibilité*)—that is to say, of pure charity; and I shall note in passing that an ascending dialectic of creative fidelity corresponds to the dialectic of hope to which I have already referred.

The notion of availability is no less important for our subject than that of presence, with which it is bound up.

It is an undeniable fact, though it is hard to describe in intelligible terms, that there are some people who reveal themselves as "present"—that is to say, at our disposal—when we are in pain or in need to confide in someone, while there are other people who do not give us this feeling, however great is their goodwill. It should be noted at once that the distinction between presence and absence is not at all the same as that between attention and distraction. The most attentive and the most conscientious listener may give me the impression of not being present; he gives me nothing, he cannot make room for me in himself, whatever the material favours which he is prepared to grant me. The truth is that there is a way of listening which is a way of giving, and another way of listening which is a way of refusing, of refusing *oneself*; the material gift, the visible action, do not necessarily witness to presence. We must not speak of proof in this connection; the word would be out of place. Presence is something which reveals itself immediately and unmistakably in a look, a smile, an intonation or a handshake.

It will perhaps make it clearer if I say that the person who is at my disposal is the one who is capable of being with me with the whole of himself when I am in need; while the one who is not at my disposal seems merely to offer me a temporary loan raised on his resources. For the one I am a presence; for the other I am an object. Presence involves a reciprocity which is excluded from any relation of subject to object or of subject to subject-object. A concrete analysis of unavailability (*indisponibilité*) is no less necessary for our purpose than that of betrayal, denial or despair.

Unavailability is invariably rooted in some measure of alienation. Say, for instance, that I am told of some misfortune with which I am asked to sympathise: I understand what I am told; I admit in theory that the sufferers deserve my sympathy; I see that it is a case where it would be logical and just for me to respond with sympathy; I even offer my sympathy, but only with my mind; because, when all is said and done, I am obliged to admit that I feel absolutely nothing. Indeed, I am sorry that this should be so; the contradiction between the indifference which I feel in fact and the sympathy which I know I ought to feel is humiliating and annoying; it diminishes me in my own eyes. But it is no use; what remains in me is the rather embarrassing awareness that, after all, these are people I do not know—if one had to be touched by every human misfortune life would not be possible, it would indeed be too short. The moment I think: After all, this is only a case, No. 75,627, it is no good, I can feel nothing.

But the characteristic of the soul which is present and at the disposal of others is that it cannot think in terms of *cases*; in its eyes there are *no cases at all*.

And yet it is clear that the normal development of a human being implies an increasingly precise and, as it were, automatic division between what concerns him and what does not, between things for which he is responsible and those for which he is not. Each one of us becomes the centre of a sort of mental space arranged in concentric zones of decreasing interest and participation. It is as though each one of us secreted a kind of shell which gradually hardened and imprisoned him; and this sclerosis is bound up with the hardening of the categories in accordance with which we conceive and evaluate the world.

Fortunately, it can happen to anyone to make an encounter which breaks down the framework of this egocentric topography; I know by my own experience how, from a stranger met by chance, there may come an irresistible appeal which overturns the habitual perspectives just as a gust of wind might tumble down the panels of a stage set—what had seemed near becomes infinitely remote and what had seemed distant seems to be close. Such cracks are repaired almost at once. But it is an experience which leaves us with a bitter taste, an impression of sadness and almost of anguish; yet I think it is beneficial, for it shows us as in a flash all that is contingent and—yes—artificial in the crystallised pattern of our personal system.

But it is, above all, the sanctity realised in certain beings which reveals to us that what we call the normal order is, from a higher point of view, from the standpoint of a soul rooted in ontological mystery, merely the subversion of an order which is its opposite. In this connection, the study of sanctity with all its concrete attributes seems to me to offer an immense speculative value; indeed, I am not far from saying that it is the true introduction to ontology.

Once again a comparison with the soul which is not at the disposal of others will throw light on our subject.

To be incapable of presence is to be in some manner not only occupied but encumbered with one's own self. I have said in some manner; the immediate object of the preoccupation may be one of any number; I may be preoccupied with my health, my fortune, or even with *my inward perfection*. This shows that to be occupied with oneself is not so much to be occupied with *a particular object* as to be occupied in a *particular manner*. It must be noted that the contrary of this state is not a state of emptiness or indifference. The real contrast is rather between the being who is opaque and the being who is transparent. But this inward opacity remains to be analysed. I believe that it consists in a kind of obduracy or fixation; and I wonder if, by generalising and adapting certain psychoanalytical data, we would not find that it is the fixation in a given zone or in a given key of a certain disquiet which, in itself, is something quite different. But what is remarkable is that the disquiet persists within this fixation and gives it that character of constriction which I mentioned in connection with the degradation of the will. There is every reason to believe that this indefinite disquiet should be identified with the anguish of temporality and with that aspiration of man not towards, but *by* death, which is at the heart of pessimism.

Pessimism is rooted in the same soil as the inability to be at the disposal of others. If the latter grows in us as we grow old, it is only too often because, as we draw near to what we regard as the term of our life, anxiety grows in us almost to the point of choking us; to protect itself, it sets up an increasingly heavy, exacting and, I would add, vulnerable mechanism of self-defence. The capacity to hope diminishes in proportion as the soul becomes increasingly chained to its experience and to the categories which arise from it, and as it is given over more completely and more desperately to the world of the problematical.

Here at last can be brought together the various motifs and thematic elements which I have had to bring out one by one. In contrast to the captive soul we have described, the soul which is at the disposal of others is consecrated and inwardly dedicated; it is protected against suicide and despair, which are interrelated and alike, because it knows that it is not its own, and that the most legitimate use it can make of its freedom is precisely to recognise that it does not belong to itself; this recognition is the starting point of its activity and creativeness.

The difficulties of a philosophy of this sort must not be disguised. It is inevitably faced by a disquietening alternative: Either it will try to solve these difficulties—to give all the answers; in that case it will fall into the excesses of a dogmatism which ignores its vital principles and, I would add, into those of a sacrilegious theodicy, or else it will allow these difficulties to subsist, labelling them as mysteries.

Between these two I believe that there exists a middle way—a narrow, difficult and dangerous path which I have tried to discover. But, like Carl Jaspers in his *Philosophy of Existence*, I can only proceed in this kind of country by calling out to other travellers. If, as it occasionally happened, certain minds respond—not the generality, but this being and that other—then there is a way. But, as I believe Plato perceived with incomparable clarity, it is a way which is undiscoverable except through love, to which alone it is visible, and this brings us to what is perhaps the deepest characteristic of that realm of the meta-problematical of which I have tried to explore certain regions.

A serious objection remains to be mentioned. It will perhaps be said: All that you have said implies an unformulated reference to the data of Christianity and can only be understood in the light of these data. Thus we understand what you mean by presence if we think of the Eucharist and what you mean by creative fidelity if we think of the Church. But what can be the value of such a philosophy for those who are a-Christian—for those who ignore Christianity or who do not accept it? I would answer: it is quite possible that the existence of the fundamental Christian data may be necessary *in fact* to enable the mind to conceive some of the notions which I have attempted to analyse; but these notions cannot be said to depend on the data of Christianity, and *they do not presuppose it*. On the other hand, should I be told that the intellect must leave out of account anything which is not a universal data of thinking as such, I would say that this claim is exaggerated and in the last analysis, illusory. Now, as at any other time, the philosopher is placed in a given historical situation from which he is most unlikely to abstract himself completely; he would deceive himself if he thought that he could create a complete void both within and around himself. Now this historical situation implies as one of its essential data the existence of the Christian fact—quite independently of whether the Christian religion is accepted and its fundamental assertions are regarded as true or false. What appears to me evident is that we cannot reason to-day as though there were not behind us centuries of Christianity, just as, in the domain of the theory of knowledge, we cannot pretend that there have not been centuries of positive science. But neither the existence of Christianity nor that of positive science plays in this connection more than the role of a fertilising principle. It favours the development of certain ideas which we might not have conceived without it. This development may take place in what I would call para-Christian zones; for myself, I have experienced it more than twenty years before I had the remotest thought of becoming a Catholic.

Speaking more particularly to Catholics, I should like to note that from my own standpoint the distinction between the natural and the supernatural must be rigorously maintained. It will perhaps be objected that there is a danger that the word "mystery" might confuse this very issue.

I would reply that there is no question of confusing those mysteries which are enveloped in human experience as such with those mysteries which are revealed, such as the Incarnation or Redemption, and to which no effort of thought bearing on experience can enable us to attain.

It will be asked: why then do you use the same word for

two such distinct notions? But I would point out that no revelation is, after all, conceivable unless it is addressed to a being who is *involved—committed—*in the sense which I have tried to define—that is to say, to a being who participates in a reality which is non-problematical and which provides him with his foundation as subject. Supernatural life *must,* when all is said and done, find a hold in the natural—which is not to say that it is the flowering of the natural. On the contrary it seems to me that any study of the notion of *created Nature,* which is fundamental for the Christian, leads to the conclusion that there is in the depth of Nature, as of reason which is governed by it, a fundamental principle of inadequacy to itself which is, as it were, a restless anticipation of a different order.

To sum up my position on this difficult and important point, I would say that the recognition of the ontological mystery, in which I perceive as it were the central redoubt of metaphysics, is, no doubt, only possible through a sort of radiation which proceeds from revelation itself and which is perfectly well able to affect souls who are strangers to all positive religion of whatever kind; that this recognition, which takes place through certain higher modes of human experience, in no way involves the adherence to any given religion; but it enables those who have attained to it to perceive the possibility of a revelation in a way which is not open to those who have never ventured beyond the frontiers of the realm of the problematical and who have therefore never reached the point from which the mystery of being can be seen and recognised. Thus, a philosophy of this sort is carried by an irresistible movement towards the light which it perceives from afar and of which it suffers the secret attraction.

EXISTENCE AND HUMAN FREEDOM

The "Marxian Man" and the "Nietzschean Man" have been dealt with at some length elsewhere; but whether or not it will ever be possible to speak of the "Sartrean Man," it is clearly impossible to do so as yet. The work of Sartre, powerful and important as it is already, is still in the making. His system of ethics has not yet been presented. Actually I believe that the construction of this system will offer grave difficulties (I shall give my reasons for this further on); however this may be, it is impossible to speak of the "Sartrean Man" without a full knowledge of this system, as to which at present we can only make conjectures.

I should like to start by explaining in what spirit I propose to tackle my subject. To begin with, my attitude is not polemical. I consider it important, as well as, in the first place, honest, to admit fully the validity and the power of some of Sartre's premises, and I shall insist on this, perhaps at the risk of shocking some of my readers, because this seems to me the only way of establishing the basis of the critical conclusions at which I arrive.

Another preliminary point I should like to stress is this: in whatever direction we may look to-day, it is hard to escape the conclusion that we have entered upon what

Christians might describe as an eschatological age. This does not necessarily mean that the end of the world is chronologically imminent, and it would seem to me very rash to indulge in any prophecies on this subject. But what is clear is that men to-day are faced with a fact which would have been inconceivable at the beginning of this century: they know that they have it in their power to destroy the universe. Moreover, one would have to be blind not to see that, at every level of being, a clearly traceable process of self-destruction is taking place; while it is much harder to see what are the forces which can—or could if the occasion arose—keep this process in check. It is from this point which seems to me central that I should like to start my inquiry into Sartre's view of existence and of human freedom. I believe that the importance of this view should not be underestimated. This was a point of difference between me and some of my colleagues at the Sorbonne towards the end of 1943; I was told that I worried too much, that "these people" liked nothing so much as a scandal, and that, by taking them too seriously, I was playing into their hands. But I believed then, as I do now, that Sartre's philosophy was much too impressive, particularly to young people, not to be examined with the utmost seriousness and objectivity; though I admit that there is in Sartre a certain taste and propensity for scandal, but this is of secondary importance and I mention it only in passing.

As I was saying, we must begin by seeing what is valid in Sartre's premises. And for this I think it is important to avoid the temptation which besets professional philosophers to envisage his thought only in the context of other, earlier philosophies, particularly that of Heidegger, even though Sartre is the first to recognise his debt to his German forerunner. What interests us much more is the actual character of that initial experience of existence which Sartre has described with such vehemence and precision, particularly in *La Nausée*. I shall take it for granted that this experience is genuine; an account of it must form the preamble to any analysis of Sartre's anthropology, and I should like to say at once that, taken in itself, it appears to me irrefutable. Our problem—and it is a difficult problem—is to know what value to assign to it.

In what follows I shall assume Sartre's work to be unknown to my readers, although in fact, most of them are no doubt familiar with at least a part of it. It seems to me preferable to begin at the beginning, and if, at any rate in the first part of this essay, I shall refer mainly to *La Nausée*, it is because this is the most forceful expression of his personality—perhaps because it is his first book. It has, indeed, all the "impetus" which so often distinguishes the first original work of a thinker—we need only think of Nietzsche's *Birth of Tragedy*, not that it would be altogether fair to burden Sartre with this rather intimidating comparison.

La Nausée is a novel, but it is in no sense a work of fiction: there can be no doubt that the identity of the hero, Antoine Roquentin, is that of the author himself. Its profound originality lies in the fact that it shows us the genesis of an experience which was at first simply lived, then fully recognised, and which finally assumed in some sense the authority of truth itself for its subject.

From the outset, Roquentin notes certain facts, such as the following:

I am very fond of picking up chestnuts, old rags, and, particularly, pieces of paper. I like to hold them in my hands, to close my fingers over them; I could almost put them in my mouth, like a small child. Annie [his mistress] used to get furious with me for picking up in the street some heavy and sumptuous paper which was perhaps stained with filth.[1]

Yet one day, seeing a piece of paper lying on the edge of a puddle and stooping to finger its soft, tender substance, Roquentin finds that he can not do it; he can no longer do what he wants:

Objects ought not to move one, since they are not alive. They should be used and put back in their place; one lives among them, they are useful and that is all. But I am moved by them, it is unbearable. I am as frightened of coming in contact with them as if they were live beasts.

He has the same experience when, holding a pebble, he has a sensation of sickly sweetness, what he calls "nausea of the hands." It is the metaphysical nature of this nausea that the novelist undertakes to explore. The experience is renewed again and again—for instance, when he looks at the braces of Adolphe, the cashier:

They annoy me by their sheep-like stubbornness; as though, having set out to be purple, they had stopped half way without giving up their pretensions. You feel like saying to them: Go, on, be purple and don't let's talk about it. But no, they remain in suspense, obstinate in their unfinished effort.[2]

Thus *nausea* (I am now speaking in my own person) seems to be bound up in its origin with an experience of fluency—not fluidity, but fluency—in so far as what is fluent slows down and assumes a kind of soft and spurious solidity. The sensation which this suggests is admittedly repellent. To understand and to sympathise with Sartre's basic experi-

[1] *La Nausée*, p. 24.
[2] *Ibid.*, p. 36.

ence I need only recall the disgusting feeling of coming on a "gooey" lump in a *purée*. "Gooeyness" is indeed the key word, but it is, for Sartre, gooeyness on an enormous scale: only an insignificant part of what he means to convey would be grasped if it were not understood that, for him, the whole of life is, if not actually gooey, at least tending towards gooeyness. What he has in mind is a certain experience of secretions and of mucus in process of formation.

> I exist, softly, softly and lightly, lightly as air. It moves a little. There are soft, melting contacts, gentle, so gentle. There is a little bubbling water in my mouth, I swallow it, it slips down my throat—and it is again in my mouth. I have in my mouth in perpetuity a little puddle of water, whitish, discreet, brushing against my tongue. And this puddle is myself, and my tongue and my throat, they too are myself.[1]

Such an experience is difficult to intellectualise; let us say that I apprehend myself both as the secretion and the mucous membrane, or rather as the mucous membrane in process of secreting. Nothing could be less formed, less definite, and it is surely in this absence of contours that the principle of *La Nausée* resides. But further, and much more paradoxically, the same is true, for instance, of my hand:

> It drags a little, hardly at all, softly, languorously, it exists. Wherever I put it down, I cannot get rid of it, any more than I can get rid of the rest of my body, of the damp heat which stains my shirt, or of the warm fat which heaves lazily, as if it were stirred with a spoon, or of all the sensations which come and go in it, rising from my thigh to my arm-pit, or drowsing softly in their accustomed place from morning till night.

Could not all this be summed up by saying that I apprehend myself as a *prey* of existence? A comparison occurs

[1] *Loc. cit.*, p. 129.

to me (I beg my readers' indulgence if I digress and interpolate my own definitions and comments, since this is the only way of maintaining the kind of contact which is necessary in order to understand and to criticise): it is that of a man who, on waking up one morning, discovers himself to be, not, as in Kafka's story, an ant, but a whole ant-heap —not just crawling with ants, but himself the seat, the centre of this monstrous proliferation, which literally comes out of him, and which, on leaving him still remains, incomprehensibly, himself.

Can we at least say that we can escape from this horror in spirit, in thought? Nothing could be more illusory, for thought itself is an ant-heap:

> Thought is the most insipid of all, more insipid even than flesh. It pulls out endlessly and it leaves a kind of aftertaste. And then there are words inside it, unfinished words, fragments of sentences which come back again and again. . . . It is worse than all the rest because I feel responsible for it, I feel like an accomplice. Take this long, painful rumination: I exist; it is I who go on ruminating. The body, once it has started up, lives on of itself. But it is I who entertain thought. I exist. I think that I exist. Ah, it is I who gently unwind this endless streamer, this feeling that I exist.[1]

Note the role of intermediary played by an image between the actual experience of the act of thinking and the nausea which is associated with this act—this will be of importance later on. It is quite impossible that my thought should appear to me spontaneously as a kind of viscous band, like a filament of toffee or liquorice. For this to happen, my thought has to withdraw from itself and to imagine itself as it would appear if it were seen as an object. The point to

[1] *Loc. cit.*, p. 130.

note is the metaphysical connotation given to a kind of repellent consistency which is alleged to be characteristic of thought.

A few years ago, after Sartre had read a paper at my house, I suggested to him that he should make an analysis of the viscous; it seemed to me so exactly in his line. The pages which he has since devoted to this subject are altogether remarkable, and I am happy and proud to have suggested it to him.

All this becomes clear *a contrario* when it is compared with the description which Sartre gives of "Boulevard Noir," the main artery of Bouville (the action of *La Nausée* takes place in "Bouville"—probably Le Havre, where Sartre was a schoolteacher):

> A street of iron, it has not the indecent mien of middle-class streets which make up to the passers-by. . . . It is inhuman like a mineral or a triangle. It is fortunate that there should be such a street in Bouville. Usually they are only to be found in capitals, in London beyond Greenwich or in the direction of Friedrichsheim or of Neukolln in Berlin. . . .
>
> Nausea has been left behind under the yellow lights. I am happy; this cold, this darkness are so pure; am I not myself a wave of frozen air? To have no blood, no lymphatic tissue, no flesh. To flow along this canal towards that pale light. To be nothing but the cold.[1]

This frozen and liberating emptiness is contrasted with materiality of whatever kind, or rather, to be more exact, with humid materiality wherever it assumes the form of proliferation or excrescence.

This kind of materiality is experienced by Sartre not as overabundance of being but as fundamental and absurd

[1] *Loc. cit.*, p. 45.

contingency. Nausea is, at bottom, the experience of contingency and of the absurdity which attaches to existence as such. Sitting in a public garden, Roquentin has the revelation of absurdity, to begin with the absurdity of inanimate things. He is staring at a root, and this root exists in the exact measure in which he finds it inexplicable. Nobbly, inert, nameless, it fills his vision and brings him back again and again to the problem of his own existence:

It was useless to repeat to myself: This is a root; it did not click in my mind. Its function did not explain anything: there was no connection between its function as root, as hydraulic pump, and this hard compact surface, like the skin of a seal, this oily, harsh obstinacy. The function explained roots in general, but this particular root, with its colour, its shape, its arrested movement, was beneath all explanation. Every one of its qualities leaked from it a little, overflowed, became partly solid, became almost a thing; every one of them was unnecessary in a root.

This recalls the braces of Adolphe, and it is most interesting to see this unusual link emerge between braces and roots. This kind of obscene overabundance is contrasted with the linear perfection of a phrase of melody; but it must be said at once that this pure melody does not exist any more than a geometrical figure.

Make no mistake about it: it is not merely the existence of a thing—a root for instance—which is being challenged, one might almost say incriminated, but existence as such: existence as unmasked in the root, bereft of its seemingly innocuous, abstract, categorical mien, and revealed in its terrifying and obscene nudity. I apologise for the continuous recurrence of this adjective, obscene; it is the right word, and we shall see the reason for it more and more clearly as we go on.

All these things—the chestnut trees, the bandstand, the statue by Velleda in the laurel thicket—abandoned themselves to existing like those tired women who relax into laughter murmuring in a tired voice: "It is good to laugh." I saw that there was no half way between non-existence and this swooning overabundance. If you exist at all, you have to exist to this point: to the point of swelling, of mouldering, of obscenity.

Note the comparison which is meant to underline this loose, unbuttoned excess. What could be further than this from the traditional vision of the overabundance of being which has haunted all the great poets, particularly the pantheists from Lucretius to Maurice de Guérin? The overflowing richness of reality which was experienced by them as something positive, and as a kind of glory, is for Sartre a looseness, an obscenity (the word is inevitable). And let there be no mistake: man himself is part of this looseness:

There we were, the whole lot of us, awkward, embarrassed by our own existence, having no reason to be here rather than there; confused, vaguely restless, feeling superfluous to one another. Superfluity was the only relationship I could establish between these trees, these hedges, these paths. Vainly I strove to compute the number of the chestnut trees, or their distance from the Velleda, or their height as compared with that of the plane trees; each of them escaped from the pattern I made for it, overflowed from it or withdrew. And I too among them, vile, languorous, obscene, chewing the insipid cud of my thoughts, I too was superfluous. [I is you or I or anyone.] Luckily I did not feel it, I only understood it, but I felt uncomfortable because I was afraid of feeling it. . . . I thought vaguely of doing away with myself, to do away with at least one of these superfluous existences. But my death—my corpse, my blood poured out on this gravel, among these plants, in this smiling garden—would have been superfluous as well. I was superfluous to all eternity.

We are in the full glare of the absurd.

Absurdity was not an idea in my head nor the sound of a voice, it was this long, dead, wooden snake curled up at my feet, snake or claw or talon or root, it was all the same. Without formulating anything I knew that I had at last found the clue to my existence, to my nausea, to my life. And indeed, everything I have ever grasped since that moment comes back to this fundamental absurdity.

Such is the revelation, the negative enlightenment. Mark this particular combination of words, for it is the clue to much of Sartre's work. It is because Sartre's enlightenment is negative that his philosophy is, in the last analysis, a philosophy of non-being. No doubt it may be questioned if enlightenment can indeed be negative: to say enlightenment is to say light, and absurdity is opacity itself, it is the contrary of what gives light. If there is any light in it, it can only come from myself, in so far as it is a self which is set up in opposition to reality, but this kind of self is, etymologically, *eidolon*—idol. Thus we clearly perceive the important truth that Sartre's thought is eidolocentric.

I have said thought, not wisdom. According to Sartre, what men commonly call wisdom or experience is most likely to be a deliberate way of lying to oneself and of concealing the fundamental absurdity which is existence itself. The following passage from *La Nausée* illustrates this view; it is a passage which I personally greatly admire, though not without reservations. Monsieur Achille is sitting in a *café* sipping his *Byrrh*:

His face is handsomely wrinkled: it has the vertical bars, the crow's feet, the bitter lines on either side of his mouth, not to count the yellow strings which hang down under his chin. He has clearly been fortunate: it stands out a mile that he has suffered and lived. And indeed he deserves his face: at no moment of his life has he been in any doubt as to how to use his past, and now he has stuffed it and hands it out as experience for the use of ladies and young men.[1]

Who, then, are these V.I.P.'s, these professionals of experience?

They have dragged out their lives in drowsiness and half-sleep. They have scurried into marriage and they have conceived children by chance. They have met other men in *cafés* and at weddings and funerals. Now and then they have been caught in a whirlpool and have struggled to understand. But everything that went on around them began and ended out of their sight. Long obscure shapes, events coming from afar brushed swiftly against them and were gone before they could look round. Then, in the forties, they put together their little obstinacies and a few proverbs, they label this experience and they turn themselves into penny-in-the-slot machines: the slot on the right is for anecdotes wrapped in silver paper, the slot on the left is for valuable advice which sticks to your teeth like gum.

Their advice is to make the least possible noise, to live as little as possible and to allow oneself to be forgotten. The best stories are about eccentrics and rash people who have been caught and chastised. "Yes, that's how things are and nobody can deny it."

Further light on this is shed in the chapter which describes Roquentin's visit to the Museum of Bouville. A recently acquired picture hung over the entrance of the Bordurin-Renaudas gallery:

It was signed by Richard Severin and it was entitled "A Bachelor's Deathbed." Naked to the waist, the torso a little green as befits a corpse, the bachelor lay prone on an untidy bed; the disordered blankets and sheets showed that the agony had

[1] *Loc. cit.,* p. 92.

been long and painful. . . . This man had lived for himself alone, his punishment—a lonely deathbed—was as severe as it was deserved. This picture was a warning to me to retrace my steps while there was still time. And if I disregarded it I was to remember this: with the exception of the Reverend Mother of an orphanage and of a few young men whose premature deaths were mourned by their families, there was not a single celibate among all the hundred and fifty notables whose portraits hung on the walls of the great gallery which I was about to enter. Not one of them had died without leaving children and a will; not one of them had died without the last sacraments. On good terms with God and the world on that day as on all the others, these men had gone to claim the part of eternal life to which they had a right. For these men had had a right to everything: to life, to work, to wealth, to obedience, to respect and now finally to eternal life.[1]

Nowhere more than in these pages does Sartre reveal his resentment against all that is implied by "social order," and perhaps also by order as such. For clearly what is being ridiculed is quite different from mere pharisaism (if it were only that, we would have no difficulty in agreeing with Sartre); or to be more exact, all middle-class virtue is regarded as pharisaical, and indeed it may be asked since the publication of *Le Mur* and *Les Chemins de la Liberté* if all virtue (e.g. conjugal, filial, etc.), with the possible exception of courage, is not treated as middle class and consequently as *declassé* and as valueless.

I ought really to quote at length the extraordinarily biting description of the portraits of notables which adorn the Museum of Bouville. What seems to me particularly characteristic is the identification of the notable himself with his hideously academic portrait. It is as if the idea of the portrait were already contained in the idea of the notable: the notable *is* his own portrait; his very essence is to be lying and *trompe l'œil.* Every detail of this passage brings out Sartre's sympathy—and also his contempt—for the celibate as such, as well as the aversion he feels for the *paterfamilias* with his gaggle of brats. I would say at the risk of shocking some of my readers that there is in Sartre socially something of a Henri Bordeaux *à rebours,* just as in the same way there is in him, theologically, something of an inverted Bernardin de St. Pierre.

It should be noted that for Sartre the very existence of the family is profoundly suspect. This is, no doubt, partly the result of his temperament, as is borne out by an incident which I have in mind. I had suggested in conversation the idea, which I still hold, that Sartre's world is the world as seen from the terrace of a *café.* Incidentally, this remark brought upon me—or, rather, upon Fr. Troisfontaines, who repeated it—the bitterest criticism on the grounds that this was not the way to speak of a philosopher. Yet I think that we were right, and Sartre himself has recently said to Fr. Troisfontaines: I am accused of spending my life in *cafés;* it is true that I cannot work anywhere else. A *café* has the immense advantage of indifference: I and the other people who come to it are independent of one another. Just imagine, if I had a home, I could never work in it; there would be a wife, children; they would be a burden to me, and all the heavier the more they were obviously anxious not to be a burden, not to worry me. This is putting things at their best, and there are far more sinister possibilities.

But I believe personally that there is a good deal more in it than that. In addition to the fact that the family must represent for Sartre that viscous element which he particularly dislikes, I believe that the father of a family must appear to him as someone who is always playing a part. To use a formula which is not one of Sartre's, but which, I think, is Sartrian, to be a father is to be always and inevitably somebody who *acts* the role of a father; indeed, if he did not act this role he would be immèdiately accused of being an unnatural parent.

Let us stop a moment to consider this notion of play-acting. The performer inevitably performs not only for others, but also for himself; he is therefore *acting* rather than *being* what he is. But, asks Sartre, is this merely a perversion? Does it depend upon us to avoid it as a stumbling block? In his principal work he formulates this question with the utmost precision. How is it possible, he asks, to *be*, while, as it were, being at the same time the consciousness of one's being? Does not consciousness of being imply a gap, a space, which prevents the perfect coincidence of a being with it-self, and therefore prevents any true simplicity void of all posturing?

All this may seem rather abstract, but the following analysis will enable us to understand the issue.

To get down to principles, what manner of being should be attributed to a being who exists for himself—that is, to a being who is conscious of his own existence? This kind of being is regarded by Sartre as something altogether different from that of being-in-itself. Being-in-itself, he tells us, is completely full of itself, it is purely and simply what it is; it has no inwardness and, consequently, no potentiality and no future. It can never be in the relation of "other" to an-other being; indeed, it can have no relationship with An-other. It is itself, indefinitely and without any possibility of being anything else. We need not ask at this point if this view of being-in-itself is real or mythical, nor if the author is justified in speaking of positivity in this context. The important point is that, in contrast with being-in-itself, being-for-itself is defined as not being what it is.

The characteristic of consciousness, Sartre tells us, is that it is a decompression of being. It is of the essence of conscious being to be what it is not and not to be what it is. The being of humanity is such that it is able to adopt a negative attitude in regard to itself. Thus, to prohibit something is to "deny some future transcendence." ("Transcendence" is a term which is overworked by Sartre who, like his predecessors, means by it merely something which transcends my immediate circumstances.) This denial is something different from a mere statement.

My consciousness constitutes itself in my flesh as the annihilation (*néantisation*) of a possibility which is projected by another human consciousness as its own.

To understand what is meant by this jargon, let us take an example. Suppose that I say to my son, "No, you are not to be an actor" or "I won't let you be a dirt-track racer," I deny being to these possibilities which he had planned for himself. This denial is what Sartre means by *néantisation*. There are even some people—guards, overseers, he observes, whose entire social function is to be a *no*. They will have lived and died without ever having been anything but a "Thou shalt not." Clearly the function of a gaoler is to incarnate "Thou shalt not escape," and it is indeed melancholy to think that a human destiny can be reduced merely to this.

There are other forms of negation which are more inward such as irony or resentment. But all these attitudes are only made possible by a certain universal structure of being-for-itself, which is, at is were, alloyed with non-being. We are told that conscious being is present to itself; but we are not to see in this the sign of an ontological dignity, as would have been held, for instance, by Pascal. From Sartre's standpoint, presence is inferior to coincidence, because presence implies a separateness.

Once again we see how Sartre's thought is dominated and, as it were, hypnotised by a given image. Let us imagine two leaflets placed exactly one on top of the other; this is coincidence. Now imagine that the leaflets have become slightly detached: this will correspond to *less being* as compared with coincidence, which was perfect and, as it were, ideal. We have seen that consciousness is a decompression of being. But if we ask ourselves what it is that separates a subject from itself, we shall be obliged to say that it is precisely *nothing*. In general separation is created by distance or the passage of time; but nothing separates, for example, the consciousness of a belief from the belief itself, since the belief is nothing other than the consciousness of the belief. Yet the fissure is there, it is intraconscious, but it will come to the surface as bad faith. Thus we come back to the concept of being as impersonation.

To make this clearer, let us follow one of those analyses of concrete examples in which Sartre excels, but from which he seems to me to draw quite unwarranted conclusions. It is just as if there were a "leakage" somewhere; and nothing is more important in a work of this sort, once we have established the validity of the premises, than to track down this "escape."

The example is that of a woman who goes for the first time to keep an appointment with a man, knowing what are his intentions in regard to herself. She knows that she will have to make a decision sooner or later, but she prefers to put it off; she deliberately concentrates on the proofs of discretion and respect which her partner has given her. She confines herself to what the relationship is at the moment, without thinking of the further plans by which it is governed in his mind. In other words, the man is, for her, a charming and agreeable companion; as for what he keeps in the back of his mind, she discounts it, because clearly, if she thought about it, she would have to alter her attitude; she would have to be more reserved and less responsive to so much charm.

So she affects to regard the man as sincere and considerate in exactly the same way as a table is round or square; she treats his qualities as though they were permanently fixed, like the qualities of things. This is because she is not quite clear about what she wishes; she is deeply moved by the desire she has aroused, but if this desire were crude and unconcealed, she would feel humiliated and repelled.

To use terms which are not exactly those of Sartre, she establishes a relationship with the man by which she manages to deceive herself.

Now she allows her hand to be held; it lies inert between his warm hands, neither consenting nor resisting—it is a thing. She conceives herself as not being her own body, but at seeing it from above, as though it were a passive object at the mercy of happenings which it can neither provoke nor prevent, since they are outside itself.[1]

In this instance, bad faith consists in a certain act of holding contrary notions which combine an idea with its opposite.

But all this is only made possible by the peculiar structure

[1] *L'Etre et le Néant*, pp. 57–8.

of the human being which continually obliges each one of us to *make ourselves* what we are. It is our manner of existence to *have to be what we are.*

Look at this waiter who is serving us. His gestures are lively, insistent and a little too precise. He comes to get his orders a little too quickly, he bends down a little too readily; his voice, his glance are a little too solicitous. Now he is coming back with the drinks, imitating in his walk the inflexible rigour of an automaton, carrying his tray with agility of a conjurer, keeping it in a state of precarious equilibrium which he restores by a flick of his wrist and arm. His whole manner is a performance. His movements are linked together like the parts of a mechanism, even to his expression and his voice; he affects the incredible neatness and swiftness of inanimate objects. He is play-acting, he is enjoying himself; what then is his role? Whom is he impersonating? The answer is simple: he is impersonating a waiter in a *café*.[1]

Now suppose that I am this waiter. I shall have to say that I am trying to achieve the being-in-itself of a waiter in a *café*. As though indeed it were not in my power to confer value and urgency upon my rights and duties of state; as though I were not at liberty to get up every morning at five or to stay in bed at the risk of being dismissed; as though, by the very fact of keeping up this role, I were not transcending it and, as it were, establishing a domain outside my condition as waiter. Yet it is beyond doubt that I am, in a sense, a waiter and not a diplomat or a journalist. But this cannot be true after the manner of being-in-itself, but only after the manner of being that which I am not; and this is true of every one of my attitudes and of my ways of behaving. Perpetually absent from my body and from my actions, I am, despite myself, that "divine absence" as it is

[1] *Ibid.*, p. 100.

termed by Valéry. I cannot even say that I am here or that I am not here in the same sense as I say that this box of matches is, or is not, on this table.

This requires some elucidation. To go back a little: is the waiter a waiter by his essence, in the same way as he is, for instance, a male, born under such and such conditions? Evidently not. He is a waiter in the sense that *he has to be* a waiter, that he earns his living by fulfilling this role, and this is obviously true of many other kinds of function. Similarly, it is curious but profoundly true that I cannot say "I am here" or "I am not here" in the sense in which I say that this box is, or is not, on this table. I am here and yet I escape this mode of being on every side. I am, as it were, "in transit," as one who has just come and is about to leave. I am here because I have to be here and not by virtue of my essence.

But Sartre's analysis goes further still and it is here that it falls into sophistry.

I "am" sad. But is not this sadness myself in the sense that I "am" what I am? Sadness is indeed the meaning of my mournful looks, of my hunched-up shoulders and of my bowed head. Yet, in the very act of assuming these postures, do I not know that I need not assume them? That, if a stranger came in suddenly, I would raise my head and change my expression; and what would be left of my sadness except the appointment I had made with it for a little later on, after my visitor has left? To be sad is to make oneself sad. . . . If I *make* myself sad I cannot *be* sad (in the sense in which a stone is heavy). The being of sadness escapes in and through the very act by which I assume it. The being-in-itself of sadness haunts my consciousness of being sad, but only as an unattainable ideal; it is an indication of my sadness but not its constituent modality.[1]

[1] *Loc. cit.*, pp. 100–1.

I may be able to show the sophistry of this argument by an illustration to which the above passage rigorously applies. Suppose that I am going to the funeral of an acquaintance; I am sorry that he has died, but I am not moved at all deeply. Yet as I come into the house of mourning I am affected by its sadness. Indeed, I wish to some extent to be affected by it so as not to be out of tune with the bereaved family whom I have come to visit. I shall therefore not merely assume an outward deportment, saying to myself: "Now I must cast down my eyes and heave a deep sigh"; I shall make a real effort (which indeed shows my natural bad faith) to think of the event as genuinely sad. I shall perhaps say to myself: "Poor gentleman, he might have lived another twenty years and enjoyed seeing his grand-children," or "After all, he was not so much older than my-self" or else "The same accident might have happened to Uncle So-and-so," so that by a kind of active goodwill I shall really succeed, as Sartre says, in feeling sad while knowing that in a moment, when I leave this house, I shall sigh with relief and dismiss my sadness like a cab.

All this is quite true, but just because it is true, it is easy to see that it is only part of the truth, and that to identify this kind of feeling with a genuine and profound grief can be only a bad joke. Note that there is a form of experience which, at least superficially, seems to bear out Sartre's view. Suppose that I am deeply grieved by the death of a friend and that someone calls on me who did not know my friend, and in whom I do not wish to confide. It may well be that I shall find in me the strength to control myself, and to ap-pear to talk naturally about the weather or about politics. But does this mean that I have packed up my grief and deposited it like a parcel in the cloakroom? Not in the least;

I remain profoundly grieved; sadness is still in the depth of my consciousness as something genuine and vivid which underlies the attitude I have adopted merely in order to conform to a social code.

This example may show how it is possible to start from a profoundly true and just observation and, by pushing it to its limit, to arrive at a conception of human life and sensibility which is not only false, but odiously offensive and degrading.

There are other cases, according to Sartre, in which people refuse to be what they are for fear of being confined to a form of being-in-itself which would deprive them of their freedom. Once again his analysis is remarkable; I apologise for using his unsavoury but highly characteristic illustration. It often happens that a pervert, while admitting every individual fault which he has committed, yet refuses to admit that he is a homosexual. He insists that his case is different from all others, that there is in it an element of chance, of ill-luck, that it should be seen as the effect of a restless seeking rather than of a deeply rooted tendency. His bad faith irritates the friend in whom he confides, and who urges him to recognise himself for what he is. But, says Sartre, who is in bad faith, the homosexual or the advocate of sincerity? The former admits his faults, but he does not wish to be regarded as a thing, which is what it is. His standpoint includes a right understanding of truth, but life forces upon him a continual evasion, and so he tends towards a different interpretation of the term "being." What he means by "not being" is not being-in-itself. Yet in asserting that he "is not" a homosexual he appears in fact to use these words in exactly the same sense as if he were to say that this table "is not" an inkstand; he is therefore in bad faith. Yet, on the other hand, does not the champion of sincerity imply that if the homosexual admitted that he was a homosexual he would immediately deserve indulgence?

Now what can this possibly mean if not that the man who admits himself to be a homosexual escapes by this very act into the domain of liberty and goodwill and ceases to be the homosexual he admitted himself to be? He is asked to be what he is in order to cease being what he is; he is required to constitute himself as a thing precisely in order to cease being regarded as that thing.[1]

This is where we come to another dangerous equivocation. Is not this contradiction, says Sartre, precisely what makes up the need for sincerity? Is not the need for sincerity itself rooted in bad faith? At bottom, when I admit that I am what in fact I am, is it not in the secret hope of being somehow delivered by this confession from being what I am?

We cannot go on to a deeper analysis of this suggestion without making this simple point: if sincerity itself is a manifestation of bad faith, then bad faith cannot exist. Bad faith cannot be defined, it cannot assume its specific character except by opposition to sincerity. If sincerity is a form of bad faith, what is left of bad faith?

But there is another and more serious point. Sartre claims that the admission that we have this or that characteristic—say that we are greedy or deceitful—is a manner of ridding ourselves of that characteristic itself. "If I admit that I am a liar I shall be a liar a little less; by the very fact of saying it I shall cease to be a liar to the same extent." This may be true of some cases (everything is true in psychology, and it is because everything is true that there is room for so much

[1] *Loc. cit.*, pp. 103–4

error). But what is serious is that Sartre leaves out of account the extremely important fact that, when a man who is in good faith admits that he is, say, a homosexual or a liar, all he does is to lay down the conditions which, in his estimation, might enable him to transform himself. Clearly, if I do not admit that I am a liar, I have no chance at all of correcting this defect, whereas if I do admit it, there is at least some possibility that I might make an effort in this direction.

What Sartre does not see, or perhaps does not wish to see (for it is always risky to accuse so prodigiously intelligent a writer of being blind), is that sincerity should not be regarded as a virtue for its own sake (a good deal of confusion has been caused in this domain by Gide, and Sartre's position is even more extreme); it is a virtue only as the necessary condition of a certain inward effort at self-mastery, shall we say at transcendence, using this word in a truer sense than that in which it is used by Sartre. I mean that when I admit that I have this or that defect, I place myself in a new position in which the overcoming of that defect may perhaps be possible.

This should be enough to show how impossible it is to maintain Sartre's opposition between "being-for-itself" and "being-in-itself"; this will become clearer still as we go on to examine the question of the relationship between the self and others, which is a crucial problem. How can I really become aware of others as others? Once again, Sartre's initial observation is penetrating and valid.

I am walking in a public garden (*L'Etre et le Néant*, pp. 311, *et seq.*). Not far from me is a lawn and alongside it there are some chairs. I see a man walking towards them and I become aware of him simultaneously as an object and as a man. In so far as he is a thing, a mannequin, a doll, I am aware of him only as being at a certain distance from the edge of the lawn and from this or that chair.

This is perfectly true, it is possible to imagine a sort of preliminary stage of awareness in which the man at a distance appears to me rather like a silhouette at the end of a shooting gallery. If I were a madman without any consciousness of the human reality of this being, I might say: "Hullo, I shall take a shot at this moving target." Clearly I would not regard this "target" as "someone else"; it would be merely a moving object and I would want to know if it was within the range of my gun. Such an attitude obviously falls short of an awareness of others; it is concerned merely with a series of metrical relations—the variable but measurable distance between the gun and the target, or the target and the chairs and the lawn—it has nothing to do with the relationship between human beings. But all this is changed the moment I say to myself: "Hullo. It is not a moving object; it is a man." At this point, says Sartre, all the inanimate objects—the lawn, the statue, the bandstand, the chairs—appear to me to be pulled over there, towards that individual who is looking at them. To use a simile which is not one of Sartre's, but which I think explains what he means, each one of us uses his consciousness like a kind of drag-net in which, as it were, to catch everything he sees; consequently, that other over there, using his drag-net to pull the statue and the lawn to himself, is, in a sense, my adversary and my rival. "The appearance of others coincides with a kind of frozen landslide of the universe, or with a shifting of its centre which undermines the centralisation operated by myself. . . . It is as if the world had a sink-hole in the middle and were continually emptying itself through that hole."

(The expression is inelegant, but characteristic.) Because of this the other will appear to me, by definition, as a menace, as threatening to dispossess me of that world of which, hitherto, I alone was the centre.

Suppose that all the chairs in the garden are taken with the exception of one on which I intend to sit down; the "other" is also looking at it and the mere fact that he too is conscious of the chair as something on which to sit down starts a sort of struggle between us, like the rivalry between two guests who covet the remaining cake at a party. But all this is nothing to what happens when the "other" is, for me, a subject.

Sartre's analysis is once more masterly. The relationship which might be termed "being seen by another" is a fact which cannot be deduced from the essence either of myself as subject or of the "other" as object. There is perhaps nothing more remarkable in the whole of Sartre's work than his phenomenological study of the "other" as looking and of himself as exposed, pierced, bared, petrified by his Medusa-like stare. My subjective reactions to this form of aggression are, in the first place, fear (the sense of being endangered by the liberty of another), and, secondly, pride or shame (the sense of being at last what I am, but at a distance from myself, for another who is over there). Not to take up too much space, I will not quote at length the passage in *Sursis* in which Daniel realises that he is seen, that there is a cosmic gaze watching him, and is converted by this realisation. It is hard to tell whether Sartre believes in the genuineness and permanence of this conversion, but there is something highly characteristic about the incident. To understand it, we must recall the shock experienced on discovering that we are being watched at a moment when we had thought that we were alone. I wish I could quote the rather embarrassing page in *L'Etre et le Néant* in which Sartre describes himself as hearing the approach of footsteps just as he is kneeling down outside a door eavesdropping and peering through the keyhole. "Nailed to the spot" is the right expression to convey the feeling of being caught and, as it were, immobilised in the act. But it is not by chance that this example has been chosen by Sartre and its speciousness is evident. Eavesdropping is not an activity ordinarily pursued in public; if I indulge in it, I expect to be alone; this is my postulate and I take it for granted that I do not run the risk of being found out. But it remains to be seen whether this is true of human life as a whole. Clearly for Sartre, the awareness of others is inseparable from the shock of the encounter with what he describes as a "freedom," an alien freedom which is adverse and threatening to himself. To the question: In what way is it menacing? Sartre replies: "because it tends to confine me within being-in-itself. In the eyes of the other I sit on this chair in exactly the same way as that inkpot stands on that table, I bend down to peep through the keyhole in exactly the same way as a tree is bent by the wind. To be seen is to be at the mercy of a freedom which is not my own ·The sense of shame is bound up with the sense of falling into the world."

"Falling into the world" signifies that I am torn out of myself, that I am dispossessed; it is this dispossession which is brought about by the gaze of another. This gaze will stigmatise me as an eavesdropper. The social consequences of such a scene are, of course, embarrassing, but they are not the crux of the matter.

We are here at the root of the diabolical argument which is developed in *Huis Clos*. I was recently told of an ingenuous comment by a manufacturer from the north, who, after seeing the play in Paris, said to his confessor: "You told me Sartre was an atheist; but he believes in the doctrine of Hell; the action of *Huis Clos* takes place in Hell." The good man was quite comforted. But alas! the Hell of *Huis Clos* is a very earthly Hell. It is, so to say, the condition of mankind carried to a paroxysm. As Mr. Campbell notes in his book on Sartre: "Sartre has achieved a hellish situation by depriving the mind of those avenues of escape which are ordinarily at its disposal. By putting together a weakling, a dæmoniac and a woman of no importance [the description is apt] he has constituted a trio which is bound to function as badly as possible."

Mr. Campbell, whose analysis of the play is remarkable, makes the apt and amusing observation that deceit is a form of behaviour between two people: it is a manifestation of intimacy. It is indeed much more difficult to tell a lie before a third party; his presence is paralysing. Now, in *Huis Clos* each one of the characters in turn represents this *terzo incommodo*, to quote Stendhal; each one is a torturer for the two others (a torturing Medusa); in fact, it is this "third" who constitutes their Hell. Inevitably, little by little, the unwelcome truth will out, and, as will be remembered, the truth is particularly abject in this case: the man, Garcin, is a deserter, Ines is a Lesbian, guilty of the death of her friend's husband, and Estelle has an infanticide on her conscience. Mr. Campbell believes that their Hell would have been no less hellish if Garcin had been a victorious general, Estelle a virtuous wife and mother, and Ines a Carmelite. This remains to be seen; the play would certainly have had an added interest. According to him, Sartre has weakened his case by making an unnecessary concession to the audi-

ence, whose susceptibilities would have been shocked by
the sufferings of a general and a Carmelite, and whose
hopes of Heaven are strengthened by seeing a deserter in
Hell. But all this seems to me in the nature of a joke, and
I believe the truth to be different. Sartre, who is an extremely intelligent writer, saw that his play would be difficult to construct with irreproachable characters. However
this may be, the play bears out what we have already observed in connection with "being seen"—the tendentious-
ness of Sartre's reasoning, which in the end becomes so
marked that we are forced to ask ourselves what lies at the
root of the prejudice which infects the whole of his work.

What, in fact, is Sartre's approach to the theory of the
awareness of others? Its whole tendency is to assert that
human communication is doomed to failure; that the sense
of community—the sense of forming part of a *we*-subject—
is only experienced on such occasions as when a regiment is
marching in step or a gang of workmen is pulling together,
circumstances where the rhythm is in fact produced by myself and happens to coincide with that of the concrete community of which I am a member. But when it comes to the
genuine community, the community of love or of friendship, Sartre's analysis of love in *L'Etre et le Néant* and,
still more, the illustrations of that analysis in *L'Age de
Raison*, reveal the fundamental agnosticism and even nihil-
ism of his view.

Sartre's analysis of love is conducted in such a way that
it is bound to arrive at a wholly negative conception. The
aim of love is to appropriate the will of another,[1] not for
the sake of power, but in order to acquire absolute value in
the eyes of the beloved, and thus to transform the alien gaze

[1] *L'Etre et le Néant*, p. 434.

which had previously passed through me or had immobilised me in an in-itself.

The aim of love is to cease being seen as ugly or small or cowardly; instead of feeling that my existence is superfluous I would feel that it is upheld and willed, even in its smallest details, by an absolute will, an absolute "freedom," which is itself conditioned by my own existence and willed by my own freedom. The essence of the joy of love, in so far as it exists, is to feel that my existence is justified. As will be remembered, existence was represented as the awareness of superfluity. But now, through the miracle of successful love (in the improbable event that love can ever be successful) the sense of superfluity would be replaced by the sense that my existence is justified, that it is, as it were, snatched out of the orbit of that ultimate contingency which is, as we have seen, the fundamental principle of *La Nausée*.

But it must be said at once that this ideal is regarded as utterly unattainable. Sartre shows to what perversions, to what extremes of sadism or masochism love can give rise when it does not sink into indifference or degenerate into hate. Incidentally, each of these by-products carries with it a duality which tends to dissolve it. It would be too long to go into details, but an important point is that the death of the beloved does not resolve the problem in any sense. That which I was for the other is perpetuated by the other's death;[1] I am that irremediably in the past, and also in the present and the future to the extent that I keep to the attitudes, the plans, the way of life, which the other has judged. The death of the other constitutes me irremediably as a thing, in exactly the same way as would happen through my own death. This is why the death of Xavière in

[1] *Loc. cit.*, p. 483.

L'Invitée, by Simone de Beauvoir, resolves absolutely nothing. On the contrary, the triumph of Xavière is perpetuated by the very fact that she is killed by Françoise.

It is clear that the whole of this dialectic, with its undeniable power and agility, rests upon the complete denial of *we* as subject, that is to say upon the denial of communion. For Sartre this word has no meaning at any possible level, not to speak of its religious or mystical sense. This is because in his universe, participation itself is impossible: this, philosophically, is the essential point. There is room only for appropriation, and this in a domain where appropriation is impracticable or where, if it is achieved, it fails of its object. Take, for instance, the case of a man who succeeds in enslaving his wife. She becomes his instrument, his thing; he can do with her what he wills. But the probable result is that this successful appropriation will destroy his love for her. She will lose all interest for him and the climax of success will prove to be the climax of failure. This truth has been seen long before Sartre; its inexorable logic cannot be escaped except by recognising that the aim of love is quite different from appropriation, that it is a communion the nature of which must be understood before the cause of the failure can be grasped.

We must now turn our attention to that "freedom" of which Sartre constantly speaks and ask ourselves in what it consists. Sartre claims in conversation that he is the only man who today can speak of the absolute because for him freedom has the value of an absolute; I can think of nothing more preposterous. What then is this freedom? His definitions of it are obscure. We must not be put off by such formulæ as that freedom is man's faculty to secrete his own non-being, or that it is man's capacity to be the foundation of himself; as in the case of existence, we must refer to his actual experience of freedom as he describes it, particularly in *Le Sursis*.

Mr. Campbell has brought out the role which "suspense" (*sursis*) plays in Sartre's philosophy. In the last analysis, it is existence itself which is in suspense, until the moment when death immobilises man in a state of being-in-itself. To exist is to be in suspense, to have the power to change, to shape the future, to be free. And this is how Mathieu, standing in the middle of the Pont Neuf, on the eve of Munich, visualises freedom:

Outside, everything is outside: the trees on the embankment, the houses turning the night pink, the frozen canter of Henri IV above my head; everything that has weight. Within me there is nothing, not even a whisp of smoke; there is no within. There is nothing. I am nothing. I am free, he said with parched lips.[1]

We are reminded of the hurricane on the Boulevard Noir. Better than the abstract jargon of *L'Etre et le Néant*, these few lines convey what Sartre means by *néantisation*. It is the idea that, by virtue of being human, I have the power to withdraw, to break with all this factitious world; but in so doing I become this break itself, I am nothing but this beyond, this "transcendence."

In the middle of the Pont Neuf he stopped and began to laugh. This freedom, in what distant places have I not looked for it; and it was so near that I could not see it; it is so near that I cannot touch it; it was nothing but myself. I am my freedom. He had hoped that there would come a day when he would be transfixed by joy, as by lightning. Now there was no lightning, no joy, only this dispossession, this void, this vertigo before his own emptiness, this anxiety lest his own transparency should for ever hide him from himself. He stretched out his hands and

[1] *Le Sursis*, pp. 285 *et seq.*

moved them slowly along the stone balustrade. . . . But just because he could see them they were not his own, they were the hands of another, they were outside, like the trees, like the reflections trembling on the Seine, they were cut off.

He closes his eyes and his hands become his own again.

Now along the warm stones there was nothing but a little acrid and familiar taste, ant-like and quite negligible. My hands —the inappreciable distance which reveals these things to me and for ever separates them from myself. I am nothing, I have nothing. I am as inseparable from the world as light, and I am as exiled as light, gliding over the surface of the stones or of the water, never gripped nor held. Outside, outside the world; outside the world, outside the past, outside myself: freedom is exile and I am condemned to freedom.

These words "I am condemned to freedom" should be underlined. What would they have sounded like, say, to a Descartes or to a Biran or to any other genuine philosopher of the past? surely as a most regrettable *flatus voci*. To what indeed can I be condemned? Surely it must be to a loss, to a deprivation—whether of life, of wealth, of honour or of freedom. I cannot be "condemned" to freedom unless freedom is a deprivation, a loss. And indeed, for Sartre freedom is, like consciousness, a deprivation, a defect; it is only by a kind of paralogism that he later represents this defect as the positive condition of the emergence of a world and thus bestows upon it a creative value.

To go on with our quotation from *Le Sursis*: Mathieu, face to face with his freedom, experiences a kind of vertigo. What if he should throw himself into the Seine?

Rest? Why not? This obscure suicide, this too would be an absolute. It would be a law, an ethic, a choice. It would be enough to bend down a little and the choice would be made for all eternity. . . . This act was in front of him, projected on the dark water, it was the pattern of his future. All the links with the past were cut, there was nothing in the world to hold him back, therein lay—appallingly—his freedom. . . . The water was his future. Now—it is true—I shall kill myself. All at once he decided against it. He decided that it had been only a test. He found himself standing upright, walking, slipping on the crust of a dead planet. It would be for another time.

But it is our turn to ask: what was this decision? What made it possible? By what conjuring trick is it possible to cross over from indetermination, from defect, to decision properly so called? Note first that there is no question of Sartre following the philosophic tradition which places freedom in the act of deciding:

Freedom coincides at its roots with the non-being which is at the heart of man. For a human being, to be is to choose himself; nothing comes to him either from without or from within himself that he can receive or accept. [Note this sentence, which is so heavy with meaning and with consequences.] He is wholly and helplessly at the mercy of the unendurable necessity to make himself be, even in the smallest details of his existence. Thus freedom is not a being, it is the being of man, that is to say his non-being. If we begin by conceiving of man as a fulness it becomes absurd to look in him for psychic moments or regions of freedom; we might as well look for an empty space in a vessel which we have filled to the brim. Man cannot be at times free and at other times a slave: either he is always and entirely free or he is not free at all.

This passage from L'Etre et le Néant seems to me one of the most significant and explicit in all Sartre's work. I do not believe that in the whole history of human thought, grace, even in its most secularised forms, has ever been denied with such audacity or such impudence. Having taken this step, Sartre naturally finds himself under the necessity to establish that every human action, even when it appears to be determined, is in reality free—that is to say, the result of choice. Note that for him freedom is equivalent to choice (I believe this to be a fatal error). His ideas on this subject can be summed up in a few simple propositions:—

1. Being, in the case of human beings, is equivalent to doing. Man reveals himself, under observation, as an organised unit of behaviours and comportments.

2. But the characteristic of this manner of being is its self-determination: the existence of an act postulates its autonomy (not, of course, in the Kantian meaning of this term).

3. The nature of an act is defined by its intention, and this intention always goes beyond the given actuality in its tension towards a result to be achieved—that is to say, towards a chosen end.

4. It is this end which reveals the nature of the world, and the world reveals itself for what it is in accordance with the nature of the chosen end.

5. Intention, which does not arise *out of* the given actuality but *away from* it, makes a break with what is given. This break is necessary for the awareness of what is given to be possible; it is through this that what is given can become a motivating force. It can even be said that the break is what makes the given actuality by shedding upon it the light of what does not exist as yet, that is to say of the proposed end.

6. If consciousness starts from actuality, it is only by denying it, by disengaging itself from something which already exists, to engage in the struggle for what does not exist as yet. This characteristic of being-in-itself postulates that this kind of being finds no support or assistance in its

own past. Thus, not only do we not inherit anything from others, but we do not even inherit anything from ourselves. We can never be aware of ourselves as anything but a choice which is in process of being made. Now, freedom consists simply in this fact that the choice is always unconditional.

7. Incidentally, the choice is always absurd, since it is beyond all reasons, and since it is impossible not to choose.

8. Lastly, a free intention, a free initial project is fundamental to my being; indeed it is my being itself. There exists in every one of us an initial project, which can be laid bare by the appropriate phenomenological method of existential psychoanalysis.

These propositions should really be discussed and illustrated in detail, but I must confine myself to a criticism of the most important points.

To begin with, I am inclined to think that, as on so many occasions, Sartre makes an exaggerated use of the concept of negation. "To disengage oneself from" is not the same thing as to "deny," and the term *néantisation* is highly equivocal. Let us take any one of innumerable examples. Say that a man who feels that his family life has too tight a hold on him, that he has been too cosseted and too spoilt, seeks to disengage himself from his family. This is not at all the same thing as saying that he "denies" his family. It may simply mean that he is trying to establish a free relationship in place of what had been a stranglehold. This simple example taken from everyday life shows how unsuitable and even dishonest—I can find no other word for it—is the use of the term *néantisation* with its deliberately negative associations. But there is something still more serious.

Can it be legitimate to say that, for the human being,

being is equivalent to doing? Is this not something more than a simplification? Is it not a misapprehension of what is deepest and most significant in the nature of man? How can it be right to ignore the distinction, commonly made, between what a man is and what he does? Does not this statement alone reveal the inadequacy of Sartre's ontology?

And, on the other hand, is it not plainly contrary to experience to assert that being-for-itself finds no support in its own past? Here we come back once more to the infinitely weighty question raised by what I have described as Sartre's rejection of grace in whatever form. Anybody less capable than Sartre of understanding the significance of receiving or the nature of gift cannot be conceived; it is sufficient to recall his astonishingly distorted analysis of generosity: "To give is to appropriate by means of destroying and to use this act of destruction as a means of enslaving others."[1] Gift is a means of enslaving others through the destruction of a certain object; not that this object is broken, but that it is destroyed in so far as it ceases to be mine. Does such a definition convey any genuine experience of giving? No doubt, if I had sufficient space, I could show, as in connection with sadness, that there are extreme cases to which this analysis applies, cases in which giving is used as a means of enslaving. But it is clearly impossible to generalise from this to the universal nature of giving without falling into absurdity and even into scandalous abuse.

What it comes to is this (and it is an attitude which seems to me to lay bare the roots of metaphysical pride): for Sartre, to receive is incompatible with being free; indeed, a being who is free is bound to deny to himself that he has received anything. But I wonder if here the author

[1] L'Etre et le Néant, p. 685.

of *La Nausée* does not fall into one of the worst errors which can be attributed to Idealism. Granted the many qualifications to which any statement on the history of philosophy must be subject, it is true to say that because Kant and some of his followers conceived the spirit in terms of constructive activity, they tended to make a confusion between receiving and suffering and to ascribe receptivity exclusively to matter. This is another illustration of the misleading role played by material images. As soon as the one who receives is conceived as a "recipient," the true character of receptivity is ignored. As soon as receptivity in a spiritual, or even in a living, being is confused with suffering in a material sense (in the sense in which wax suffers the imprint of a seal) it becomes impossible to conceive the concrete and organic relationship between the individual and the world. There remain only two terms of reference: an actuality which is, so to speak, inert, and a freedom which denies it only to assume it in an incomprehensible way at a later stage.

What is, at any rate, certain is that, in such a philosophy, the notion of freedom, be it even as non-being or, to use a concrete image, as an air-pocket in the midst of being-in-itself, is just as inexplicable and much more deeply unintelligible than the notion of creation which Sartre rejects and for which he has nothing but contempt. The truth is that Sartre unites the idealism of which I have spoken with a materialism which derives from the eighteenth-century tradition of French thought. Indeed, I have heard recently that one of his disciples, lecturing at Lyons, admitted this filiation and claimed this double authority in support of Sartre's teaching. But this admission brings us to a curious paradox. Existentialism (I have surely not abused this word) has developed historically as a reaction against the Hegelian system; yet it is now seen to emerge—like the tunnels on the St. Gothard railway—considerably *below* the level from which it had started. Clearly, from the standpoint of Hegel himself, the concept of being-in-itself is to be found at a very low level of dialectics. And Sartre himself constantly asserts that man is a useless passion, or that he vainly aspires to achieve in his own person the impossible synthesis which would result in being-in-itself. Man's life is an attempt, continually renewed and inevitably doomed to failure, at the divinisation of himself.

Note that this is not without truth. It is true that man seems to be irresistibly urged to confer upon himself the attributes of divinity, and the progress of technics lends a disquieting semblance of truth to the tempter's promise: *eritis sicut dii.* But the existence and the danger of this temptation are recognised the more easily the more firmly are asserted the existence and the transcendence of God. Whereas here we are, on the contrary, in the presence of explicit and aggressive atheism. It is no exaggeration to say this, for Sartre himself recently stated in conversation that his atheism was becoming increasingly militant and aggressive. There are to be found in *L'Etre et le Néant* certain rudimentary proofs of the non-existence of God which show the depth and persistence of the author's rationalism; indeed, it is perhaps by means of this very acid that his philosophy corrodes the contemporary mind. As I have mentioned earlier, it even happens to him to reason in the manner of a Bernardin de St. Pierre *à rebours,* as when he argues from certain biological phenomena of inadaptation or of teleological incoherence to the fundamental absurdity of the universe or to the non-existence of God.

But perhaps we should recall at this point the assertion made by Sartre himself of the existence in each of us of an initial pattern which existential psychoanalysis should be able to reveal. Should we not ask what is the pattern at the origin of Sartre's atheism? The answer can be only one of two things. Either he must admit that his atheism derives from an attitude of the will or from an initial resentment (as would be the case of a man who, from the very depth of his being, willed that God should not exist); such an answer would be in keeping with his doctrine, but it would destroy much of its metaphysical bearing. Or else he must take up his stand on the traditional ground of objective thought and declare that *there is no God,* as one might say that there are no people on Mars; but in that case he must give up the plane of existentialism and fall back on the most obsolete positions of traditional rationalism.

This metaphysical aspect of the problem raised by Sartre's philosophy is not, however, the one with which this paper is intended to deal. The essential question is, to my mind, whether this philosophy is not heading for the abyss into which the forces of self-destruction threaten to drive our unfortunate race. For my part, I am convinced of it and this is the crucial point on which I must insist in conclusion.

I have recently surprised and even scandalised some of Sartre's followers by classifying his philosophy among the "techniques of vilification," by which I mean techniques which result, whether deliberately or not, in the systematic vilification of man. I admit that, superficially, this would seem to be a paradox, for does not Sartre ceaselessly exalt man and his freedom in the face of the radical absurdity of the universe? But it must not be forgotten that the Fascist dictatorships, whether in Germany, Italy or elsewhere, similarly exalted "the people" and offered it a ceaseless and cheap adulation; yet what contempt did not this adulation conceal, and to what abject depth did they not reduce their citizens. I greatly fear that the relationship between Sartre and his disciples on the one hand and between them and the humanity they claim to exalt on the other may follow an analogous pattern. Etymologically, to vilify a thing is to take away its value, its price. This can be done in the case of merchandise by flooding the market, and this is just what Sartre does to freedom: he debases it by putting it on every stall. "If freedom were easy, everything would fall to pieces at once," says Pierre Bost in his remarkable recent short story, *Monsieur l'Amiral va bientôt mourir*. No doubt, Sartre would indignantly protest against the suggestion that, in his philosophy, freedom is easy. But in that case he can surely not maintain the statement which he makes in *L'Etre et le Néant* and again in *Les Chemins de la Liberté*, that "we are condemned to be free." If we are condemned to be free, then freedom must be easy. It is true that a distinction can be made between freedom and the use of freedom, but this is out of keeping with the doctrine; for we must not forget that Sartre does not regard it as an instrument which is at the disposal of man and of which he can consequently make a good or a bad use; he regards it as man's very being— or his lack of being.

So that it is only by a kind of sleight of hand that this freedom which man is and which he cannot help being, can be later converted into a freedom which he owns and of which he can make a wrong use.

This raises the whole question of values as they are conceived by Sartre. From his standpoint, values cannot be anything but the result of the initial choice made by each human being; in other words, they can never be "recognised" or "discovered." "My freedom," he states expressly, "is the unique foundation of values. And since I am the being by virtue of whom values exist, nothing—absolutely nothing—can justify me in adopting this or that value or scale of values. As the unique basis of the existence of values, I am totally unjustifiable. And my freedom is in anguish at finding that it is the baseless basis of values." Nothing could be more explicit; but the question is whether Sartre does not here go counter to the exigencies of that human reality which he claims, after all, not to invent but to reveal.

Not to deal exclusively in abstractions, let us take a concrete case. Sartre has announced that the third volume of his *Les Chemins de la Liberté* is to be devoted to the praise of the heroes of Resistance. Now I ask you in the name of what principle, having first denied the existence of values or at least of their objective basis, can he establish any appreciable difference between those utterly misguided but undoubtedly courageous men who joined voluntarily the Anti-Bolshevik Legion, on the one hand, and the heroes of the Resistance movement, on the other? I can see no way of establishing this difference without admitting that causes have their intrinsic value and, consequently, that values are real. I have no doubt that Sartre's ingenuity will find a way out of this dilemma; in fact, he quite often uses the words "good" and "bad," but what can these words possibly mean in the context of his philosophy?

The truth is that, if I examine myself honestly and without reference to any preconceived body of ideas, I find that I do not "choose" my values at all, but that I *recognise* them and then posit my actions in accordance or in contradiction with these values, not, however, without being painfully aware of this contradiction (as was clear to the ancients: *video meliora proboque, deteriora sequor*). It should perhaps be asked at this point if it is not Nietzsche who, with his theory of the creation of values, is responsible for the deathly principle of error which has crept into speculation on this subject. But although I am the last to underrate the objections to Nietzsche's doctrine, I am inclined to think that his view is less untenable than that of Sartre, for it escapes that depth of rationalism and materialism which is discernible, to me as to others, in the mind of the author of *L'Etre et le Néant*.

I would suggest in conclusion that existentialism stands to-day at a parting of the ways: it is, in the last analysis, obliged either to deny or to transcend itself. It denies itself quite simply when it falls to the level of infra-dialectical materialism. It transcends itself, or it tends to transcend itself, when it opens itself out to the experience of the suprahuman, an experience which can hardly be ours in a genuine and lasting way this side of death, but of which the reality is attested by mystics, and of which the possibility is warranted by any philosophy which refuses to be immured in the postulate of absolute immanence or to subscribe in advance to the denial of the beyond and of the unique and veritable transcendence. Not that there is anything in this which, in our itinerant condition, we can invest like a capital; this absolute life can be apprehended by us only in flashes and by virtue of a hidden initiative which can be nothing other than grace. I am, of course, thinking of the extravagantly dogmatic negativism which is common to Sartre, to Heidegger and even to Jaspers. It is true that Sartre has criticised with some force the notion of being-for-death which dominates the thought of Heidegger; but it is all too clear that there is little to choose between that view and his own, which is equally opaque. I cannot help stating once more in this connection the dilemma to which I referred earlier on: either this assertion of man's total mortality is the expression of an existential wish—and in that case it cannot be other than contingent—or else it presupposes an objective, pseudo-scientific realism in regard to death, and implies a crass materialism which belongs to the infra-existential levels of philosophy.

Sartre verbally admits this materialism: "What will you," he says, "matter is the only reality I am able to grasp." Yet I am persuaded that this negative realism, this way of cramping the spirit to the experience of the senses, while relating this experience whenever possible to behaviourist illustrations, cannot go without a corresponding devaluation of the truly human modes of existence. In this connection, I declare without hesitation, and at the risk of bringing down on myself the thunderbolts of his partisans, that it is by no means a coincidence if Sartre's work offers the most glaring display of obscenities to be found in the whole of contemporary art. It is no use talking to me of Céline—I have far much too much respect for Sartre to compare him with his wretched predecessor; nor should he be compared with Zola, who was, after all, only a healthy, naïve "naturalist," not at all a philosopher and not blessed with too much intelligence. Given that in Sartre's world man's inherence in the universe is ignored or denied and that its level is therefore infinitely below the pantheism of the Stoics or of Spinoza, it is not at all surprising that in it man should conceive of himself more and more as waste matter or as potential excrement. Whatever the third volume of *Les*

Chemins de la Liberté is like, whatever the paper garlands that Sartre picks from the literature of the *maquis* to put on his heroes' tombs, I cannot see that the substance of his doctrine is likely to alter. For such a change to be effective and not merely to be one of lighting or décor, the very principles of his philosophy would have to be revised; and nothing leads us at present to foresee the likelihood of such a revision.

And indeed we must admit that it would be an almost unheard of thing for a philosopher who has achieved his degree of notoriety and who is, if not intoxicated with success (he is too intelligent for that), at least fully engaged in pressing his advantages simultaneously in every field, to put forth the heroic effort (for it would be nothing less than that) required for a serious reconsideration of postulates which find a deep echo in his nature and, so to speak, in his psychic make-up. Everything suggests, on the contrary, that his views will harden still further. The only question is whether, at a given moment, he will not move closer to Marxism, not that the Marxists, who are ill-disposed towards him, are likely to welcome him into their ranks. This will become clear in the near future. Meanwhile, it is from the ranks of a misdirected and anarchical youth that he will, either directly or through his zealous intermediaries, recruit his disciples and, so often, his victims.

TESTIMONY AND EXISTENTIALISM

Hardly a day goes by without my being asked what is existentialism. (Usually it is a society lady who asks for this information, but to-morrow it may be my charwoman or the ticket-collector on the Underground.) It is perhaps hardly surprising that my answers tend to be evasive: I should like to say, "It is too difficult," or "It would take too long to explain"; but I realise that such answers are disappointing and should not be given too often. What I propose to do now is not so much to define existentialism as to try to throw some light on what seems to me its essence by bringing out its key notions—that is, the notions which give the clue to it from my standpoint, which, I need hardly add, is very different from that of Sartre. Sartre has himself admitted that there is a Christian version of existentialism which is not to be confused with his own; though, for my part, I think it is insufficient and even incorrect to stress its Christian character, because I believe that many people are liable to adhere to it who do not regard themselves as Christians.

The point I should like to examine first is the distinction between testimony and the statement of an observation.

What is an observation? I observe a phenomenon or something that I take to be a phenomenon, which is outside myself and which I note. I cannot help noting it—I am *obliged* to note. At the same time I see, when I think about it, that my observation does not in any way modify the phenomenon I have observed, and, moreover, that the *I* who observes is highly impersonal: the observation I have made could have been made equally well by anyone in my place. This accounts for the legitimate and no doubt proper use of such phrases, current in scientific text-books, as "It is stated" or "One observes"; the *I* is merely an indifferent specification of the indefinite pronoun.

Now let us turn to testimony. It is never, it cannot be ever *one* who bears witness; it is always and inevitably *I*, and if not myself, then another, who is yet another *I*. It is always an individual human being, with his proper identity, taking the word in its two correlated senses—the one civic (Thomas, son of Albert and Euphemia, born at Reading, domiciled at Clapton, etc.) and the other deeper, the identity, in time and beyond time, of a being who is not exhausted by immediacy. This is what brings out the contrast between testimony and observation. I can observe only what takes place before me now, *hic et nunc*. I cannot, for instance, observe that I saw and heard John Smith yesterday; at the most I can only observe that I remember, or that I believe that I remember having seen and heard. (Even this needs a qualification for it is not certain that the existence (?) of such a memory is a fact that can be observed.) But I can testify that John Smith was at the corner of Regent Street yesterday at 4 p.m.; he was bare headed, his expression was haggard, etc. I have said that I *can* testify; this means that "I am in a position to . . . ," it can also mean that "I have the right"; and the occasion might arise when I have to say further that "I *must* bear witness" in a rather different sense from the one in which I say that "I must take note." Actually, when I say, "I am obliged to note," I already leave the realm of pure observation, for I imply that I must "admit," and this brings in a reference to other people, which, as we shall see, is of the essence of testimony but is quite outside the scope of observation. I am alone with the phenomenon I observe, alone in a specific sense because I am without my identity: I am only a recording instrument, a recorder among many thousands.

The next step is to bring out the finality which is immanent in testimony.

To be a witness is to act as a guarantor. Every testimony is based on a commitment and to be incapable of committing oneself is to be incapable of bearing witness. This is indeed the reason for the preliminary oath which is administered in a law court. By taking an oath I bind myself, I give up the possibility of withdrawing myself, as it were, from what I have said; to underline this the body itself is called into play, every effort is made to ensure that the oath is a genuine and effective act, performed by me as an individual who can be discerned and identified by other people: this stocky little man with green eyes, or that long gangling fellow with the swarthy complexion.

Before whom do I commit myself—before a law court, or before something which fulfills the function of a law court: history, or posterity or the conscience of mankind? The point here is not whether these words ring hollow but that the witness always conceives of himself as standing in the presence of someone; I would say that he is essentially a-monadic. There can be no testimony on the plane of the monad; though there can be observation on this plane, even from the most subjective standpoint: I observe that I have a headache, that my shoe pinches, etc.

Should it then be said that testimony is essentially a social act? I doubt if this ambiguous term gets us any further. The point is that testimony is given before a transcendence, perhaps even before transcendence itself; but society may have nothing to do with it, unless the word is taken in a specialised and arbitrarily defined sense. To take an example, a man I know acted as witness for the defence in a recent and famous trial. It was all too clear that the transcendence before which he spoke could not be identified with the bunch of fanatics whom he had in front of him and who, so far from taking his testimony into account, rejected it with all the might of their passions. It cannot reasonably be said that this group was the embodiment of society; yet can it be claimed that "society" was there, as a wholly ideal entity, unrepresented in the court-room, yet existing, say France, perhaps a reconciled France by opposition to the France of the partisans and the factious? It is hard to define the sociological content of such a notion. The plain fact is that the witness of whom I speak, who happens to be one of the most honourable and courageous men I know, testified before his conscience, or before Truth. (To add an instructive sequel: his unpopular evidence cost him an official appointment and a salary on which his family could have lived. The moral is worth pondering; to my mind the incident is one of the countless signs of the poisoning of the public mind by Fascism and Hitlerism; but when I told the story to a friend who is a philosopher, he replied: "What an idiot! Why couldn't he keep quiet!")

To sum up our main points: my testimony bears on something independent from me and objectively real; it has therefore an essentially objective end. At the same time it commits my entire being as a person who is answerable for my assertions and for myself. This tension between the inward commitment and the objective end seems to me existential in the highest degree.

A further point is that testimony forms part of a lawsuit; it furthers an investigation. It can thus be said to be of its essence to promote a reality of which the objective data form only one element. For there is the further question of values: there can be no law suit in which values are not at stake; uniformity in insignificance is incompatible with either testimony or judgment.

In the last analysis testimony bears on an event or that part of an event which is unique and irrevocable. If the event can be reconstructed, testimony is superfluous; in that case it becomes the duty of the judge to discount what I, as a witness, have to say. In this way we come back to what we have already foreshadowed, that there is a kind of injunction: "Thou shalt bear witness." On what is it based? In the case of a particular fact the answer is simple. I was present at the time and place of an accident; I can witness that the victim crossed at an island and that the car did not slow down; my testimony will throw light on the event and will help to assess the responsibility involved. I am obliged to bear witness because I hold, as it were, a particle of light, and to keep it to myself would be equivalent to extinguishing it. Can I refuse to attend the trial because of the trouble and the waste of time or because the victim was a stranger to me?—I would be guilty of a betrayal, but against whom? Against society? but we have seen how useless to us is this term; against the victim? but betrayal presupposes a commitment and I have no commitment to this stranger whom I have seen by chance. Clearly we must go deeper into the question to uncover the roots of this seeming injunction.

We have said that testimony is always given before a transcendence, though this transcendence can be designated by different terms. Most of these terms seem to me to be rhetorical ways of evoking something to which they can no doubt be applied but which does not require them inevitably. What concerns us is the relation in which the witness stands to the world, what is the manner of belonging to it which is implied by his function.

Note that it is a role which I am largely free to reject. I can, for instance, say to the investigating magistrate that I have seen nothing, heard nothing and can tell him nothing. This is an interesting attitude. I might attempt to justify it on the grounds of scrupulous honesty: I cannot remember exactly what I have seen, it is so easy to distort the truth unwittingly, I do not know what to think and in this doubt I prefer to abstain. Besides, I prefer to keep my independence: whatever I said would be sure to be used either by the prosecution or the defence. I would be forced to take sides, a proceeding which is abhorrent to me. I wish to keep clear of the whole affair. It is true that I would like to know what will happen, but if I come to the trial it will be as a simple onlooker.

This brings us to the distinction between the onlooker and the witness, and a little reflection will show that it is a distinction between two opposite metaphysical attitudes. There are modern philosophers who try to impale us on the horns of a false dilemma by saying to us: "either you are only an onlooker, in that case you are not involved in reality; or you are an active and free being. You have nothing but the choice between these two ways, indeed you *are* nothing but this choice, or rather this way which chooses itself." But it must be asked: does not this dilemma leave out the essential factor? By adopting this standpoint, do we not forfeit all chance of understanding the essential point of our lives—the fact that we are witnesses and that this is the expression of our mode of belonging to the world?

I freely admit the danger that this suggestion, so far from throwing light on our problems, may thicken the shadows. Witnesses to what and before whom? We have said "before a transcendence," but so far from being able to discern its visage, we could not even say if it was anyone at all.

Above all, witnesses to what? To the inextricable mixture of best and worst which we find in our experience? Are we to testify to all that—to the absurdity and the horror as well as to the nobility and the greatness? And how are we to bear witness? Are we to relate, to consign, to keep a diary in anticipation of an immense law suit?

Clearly, when we put it in this way, the question loses all meaning and we must look further for the answer to the increasingly vast problem with which we are faced. Perhaps the mistake was to conceive of testimony in a way which, by objectivising it, impoverishes and distorts it, as though it were always something of which one could make a report.

Let us look at it in this way: it has happened to all of us to say of some consecrated and devoted life that such an existence is a testimony. Now, clearly, the value of such testimony is bound up with some form of fidelity which has become embodied in such a life: it may be the fidelity of a child to its parents, of a servant to his master, or it may be fidelity to a cause served until the end. The notion of fidelity can be degraded into passivity, into the expression of a kind of brutish habit; clearly this has no value. The value lies in the faithful following, through darkness, of a light by which we have been guided and which is no longer visible to us directly; indeed, it can be said that it is because there is a darkness, an eclipse, that there can be testimony—attestation.

Let us go back for a moment to the elementary form of testimony which we examined at the beginning; this, too, presupposes an eclipse since it is based on memory: I bear witness that John Smith was at the corner of Regent Street yesterday at 4 p.m.; my testimony does not begin until *after* the irrevocable disappearance of the image, or the event, or the ephemeral combination of atoms, which was John Smith's passage through a particular point of space and moment of time. I can bear witness only as "one who remembers"—I will not say as one who has memory because by treating memory as a possession I would be in danger of confusing the issues.

We are now in a position to see that testimony is based on fidelity to a light or, to use another language, to a grace received. In using this term I wish to exclude its religious connotation and to treat it simply as signifying *gift*; the point is that testimony refers to something which has been *received*. If I have myself taken part in an event, I can only certify, I cannot bear witness.

This finally brings us to the notion of receptivity, and of a receptivity which I would describe as creative; for we must discard the Kantian notion of the relationship between receptivity and spontaneity. As I have written elsewhere,

Receptivity covers a wide scale of gradations: at one end of it is "suffering," in the sense in which wax "suffers" the imprint of a seal; at the other end is giving—and even self-giving—as when we speak of a hospitable host "receiving" his friends. This kind of "reception" is entirely different from that of a vessel which is filled with an alien substance; it is a participation in a reality, in a plenitude, and a communication of oneself.[1]

To "receive" in this sense is an act, and even an art, like that of the host who brings out the best in his guest and creates a genuine communication and exchange.

This is what must be kept in mind in analysing the term "gift." To give is to give to someone. Only a being can give to another being, and it is a question whether this does not inevitably imply some form of self-gift. Even if I give a thing, if I really give it, it must be something of myself (clearly it must at any rate be mine, since I cannot give something that does not belong to me). It is this possibility of self-gift that we must examine, for we have seen that testimony implies receptivity, but a receptivity which is in no way comparable with that of a vessel which is being filled. This is a question to which modern philosophers, particularly the empiricists, have not given sufficient attention; while the idealists, obsessed with the notion of spirit as activity and constructive power, have tended to regard receptivity as a property of material things. It may be asked if the Aristotelian tradition should not be followed up on this subject.

It is not without interest at this point to refer to Sartre's astonishing interpretation of giving in *L'Etre et le Néant* (p. 684):

Gift is a primitive form of destruction. . . . Generosity is, above all, a destructive function. The frenzy of giving which comes over certain people at certain times is, above all, a frenzy of destruction; but this frenzy of destruction, which assumes the

[1] *De Rufus à l'Invocation*, p. 123.

guise of generosity is, in reality, nothing other than a frenzy of possession. All that which I destroy, all that which I give, I enjoy the more through the gift I make of it. . . . To give is a form of destruction enjoyment, of destructive appropriation. But the gift also casts a spell over the one who receives; it forces him to re-create and continually to maintain in being that self which I no longer want, which I have enjoyed to the point of annihilation, and of which nothing remains but an image. To give is to enslave. It is to appropriate by destroying and to use the destruction to enslave another.

The writer adds that "if existential psychoanalysis finds proof of generosity in a subject, it must look further for its original purpose and discover why the subject has chosen to appropriate himself through destruction rather than through creation."

I doubt if there exists a passage in Sartre's work which is more revealing of his inability to grasp the genuine reality of what is meant by *we* or of what governs this reality, that is precisely our capacity to open ourselves to others. This fantastic interpretation may, however, throw an indirect light on our problem. It is true that there exists a pathology of giving and that there are cases of moral suicide where one person abdicates and annuls himself completely for the benefit of another; but it cannot be more clear that this has nothing to do with self-gift in the sense of which we are speaking, and which is indeed the exact opposite of servitude. To give oneself is to devote or consecrate oneself to another, and no doubt simply to consecrate oneself. What are the conditions which can make such a consecration possible? To my mind they are those which also govern testimony; and it is perhaps this winding path which can bring us to the understanding of creative receptivity.

A notion which may help us at this point is that of

transmutation. To give a thing is not merely to transfer it from one place to another but to embody in it something of oneself; what is this something? Clearly the mere fact of going into a shop to buy a present does not in itself confer any intimate significance on the gift I wish to make. Apart from the money I take out to complete the transaction, what counts is my intention, my wish to give pleasure, and perhaps also the sacrifice I make of this sum by spending it on another rather than on myself. But if my intention becomes personal and finds a means of revealing itself in the object I purchase, then it becomes possible to speak of a transmutation. By virtue of my giving it, the object, which had been until then merely a neutral thing, costing so much at this or that shop, acquires a new quality, a being-for-another, not for everybody in general but for this particular person. Clearly, this being-for-another is not an objective quality of the thing; the value of my present may lie in some memory, in some event which belongs to the life of my friend, who thus receives from me a genuine communication of myself, an expression of the manner in which he is present to me. Such a communication is existential in the sense that it is quite different from the mere transmission of a thing which is meant to reach its destination unaltered. The gift, for the one who receives it, if it is really a gift, is not just one more thing added to his possessions; it exists in another dimension, which is that of testimony, since it is a gage of friendship or of love. But the condition of its existing in this dimension is that it should be recognised as existing in this way; in this sense it is like an appeal which demands a pre-determined mode of response. Think of a small child who brings you three bedraggled dandelions it has picked by the wayside; it expects you to admire them, it awaits from you a recognition of the value of its gift; and if you lose it, or put it down carelessly, or do not stop talking to express your delight, you are guilty of a sin against love. This example seems to me instructive because of the naïve and touching spontaneity of the child, and because we are free to think that things in themselves offer themselves to us in the same eager and ingenuous way.

But a further point is that the transmutation of a thing in becoming a gift has its continuation in an accretion of being in the one who receives. Can this enrichment of the soul be compared to an accretion of physical wealth? Such a comparison is misleading because this particular enrichment can be conceived only in terms of participation; it requires an action on my part, I am at liberty to reject it by refusing my recognition and my response. And it must be admitted that this is the most difficult part of my case. My claim that I am free to respond or to refuse my response can always be questioned; for are there not indigent and ungrateful natures who are deprived of the gift of responding? Just as there are others who are incapable of trust, that is to say of faith, and who are therefore unable to recognise that life is a gift and that all things are given to them? This is an immense problem. I believe it should be possible to show that the question arises in this form only in a world where the individual is totally insulated, where he is given over to his indigence and mercilessly weaned from the tradition which should nourish him and should awake in him his capacity for recognition and for gratitude; for in such a world, short of an especial grace, he is indeed doomed to see himself, like the man of Heidegger and of Sartre, as the victim of some cosmic catastrophe, flung into an alien universe to which he is bound by nothing. But should it not be the task of a sane philosophy at this time to link up with this tradition by an effort of thought which should bring out its metaphysical evidence? Nothing short of an effort of this kind seems to me to have any chance of success against a doctrine of death on which, whatever one may say, no wisdom can be built.

AN ESSAY IN AUTOBIOGRAPHY

When I recall my childhood, so carefully watched over and in some ways so confined, with its atmosphere of moral scruples and of hygienic precautions, I can see the reason why abstraction was the keynote of my early philosophical thoughts and why I was almost contemptuously hostile towards empiricism. This attitude seems to me the direct reflection of that horror of dirt and germs which had been bred in me from my earliest youth upwards. Experience, as it is mostly conceived by philosophers, was to me impure and profoundly suspect. True, there was something in this also of the need to hit back at the practical world which at every step proved to me my inaptitude and my awkwardness: on the plane of Ideas alone was I able to create a shelter from these wounding contacts of everyday life. Thus to philosophise meant for me at first to transcend. But I must make certain reservations.

Firstly, my reference to Ideas must be taken in the widest—not in the Platonic—sense. I am inclined to think that, if, in some ways, the conception of a super-sensual world influenced my whole spiritual development, it was always deeply repugnant to me to conceive this world as a universe of Archetypes. I would say now that my idea of it

tended to become less and less *optical*. It is most likely that
my passion for music helped to prevent me from imagining
this world, if to imagine is, at least in some sense, to project
a form into space; this explains the conviction of profound
truth which came to me with the discovery of Schopenhauer's theory of music.

For all that, it would be a mistake to think that abstraction as such ever appeared to me as a habitable place. If
ever I dwelt in it, it was rather as on a landing stage from
which to embark sooner or later. The idea of an aerodrome
comes into my mind now when I try to recapture these early
experiments. What I denied, rightly or wrongly, was that
experience as it is understood by empiricists could ever be a
springboard: it seemed to me that it must suck down the
spirit like a quicksand.

Doubtless this explains why I was so deeply impressed by
post-Kantian philosophy, particularly by Schelling. Fichte
irritated me by his moralising and also by the absence of
links (not sufficiently realised by himself) between the absolute and the concrete *ego*. It was this concrete *ego* which I
could not help regarding as the veritable *I*; for, when all is
said and done, did not the problem consist in understanding
its reality and its destiny? From this point of view, Hegelian-
ism inspired me with a profound mistrust, although it attracted me infinitely more than the doctrine of Spinoza, to
which I was always strangely averse; both seemed to me to
immerse the reality and the destiny of the individual into
an absolute in which they were in danger of becoming lost.
As against this, I seemed to discern, at the end of the immense journey travelled by Schelling, a light which perhaps
one day might help me to discover my own path. Was
there not an arduous way which might give access to a

higher empiricism and to the satisfaction of that need of the individual and the concrete which I felt in myself? In other words, would not experience be for me not so much a springboard as a promised land?

Perhaps all this will be clearer if I say that from my earliest years I was haunted by the theatre, which attracted me less as a spectacle than as a privileged form of expression. Naturally, my predilection for dialogue was not clear to me at the time, but I was less fond of stories or descriptions than of that form of art which conceals itself, as it were, behind the subjects whom it confronts. As I have said elsewhere, I experienced very early on a kind of intoxication, not only in conceiving characters distinct from myself but in identifying myself with them sufficiently to become their mouthpiece. It is difficult to say how I came to have this bent; one reason was, doubtless, my father's innate sense of the theatre and his incomparable way of reading plays. But I have always thought that the imaginary characters with whom I held silent conversations replaced for me the brothers and sisters whom I so cruelly missed in real life.

There is another circumstance which, I think, must have contributed to the development of my dramatic faculties. From my earliest childhood I witnessed in my family circle differences of temperament and opinion which forced me prematurely to become aware of the *insolubilia* involved even in what seem to be the most simple relationships. Nothing has helped me more to understand that there can exist, on a given plane, incompatibilities of outlook such that a truthful and fair mind can only adopt the divergent opinions each in its turn without any real hope of reconciling them by a formula. This led me, quite apart from any technical speculation, to perceive directly that there is a certain radical weakness in the faculty of judgment and that it is necessary to assume (I will not say to conceive) the existence of a domain beyond speech in which harmony can be discerned and in a sense even restored, although the *raison raisonnante* has not received that satisfaction which, perhaps unwarrantably, it claims. At the same time, music offered me an irrefutable example of the kind of supra-rational unity which I believed to be the essential function of drama to establish and to promote. This explains the bearing of the most important of my early works, the *Quartet in A sharp,* on the connection between family tragedy, music and pure thought.

But what is particularly clear to me now is that the dramatic mode of thought, dealing as it does with subjects as such—that is to say, with their reality as subjects—illustrated and confirmed in advance all that I was later to write on the purely philosophical plane concerning knowledge in its capacity to transcend objectivity. The connection between these two modes of expression did not become clear to me until fairly late—about 1930. As to why they developed in me separately and, as it were, away from each other, I would find it hard to say. I can only suppose that, if there had been inter-communication between them at an earlier stage, it would have been at the cost of what was vital and authentic in each. It is, perhaps, no coincidence that those of my plays which now seem to me the richest in spiritual content are those which show the least trace of philosophical premeditation.

There is surely something a little shocking and absurd in setting out, like counters or like anatomical specimens, those dispositions, often unformulated at the time, in which I undertook my research. Yet this seems to me the only way to account for the haphazard nature of my undertaking and for the almost formless character of my early philosophical writings. There is no doubt that dramatic work appeared to me as the way out of the labyrinth into which I had been led by my abstract thinking; through it I hoped to emerge into the light of an organised human landscape of which it was my aim to understand the structure. Nevertheless, the pattern of this landscape, as I drew it in *Seuil Invisible,* in *Quartet* or in *Iconoclaste,* was not really different from that of what I would call the subterranean region of myself, in which my thoughts struggled to understand itself and to ensure its grasp on a reality which continually eluded it. It was the problem of the nature of reality which obsessed me throughout those years of blind groping. What I wanted to know was not so much what reality is, as what we mean when we assert its existence, and when we say that it cannot be reduced to its outward appearances, or that these appearances probably conceal more than they disclose. Was this distinction between the apparent and the real ultimate and final, as Plato and the traditional Platonists seem to have believed? Or was it related to the progress of thought which, as it were, sets out its positions successively? But if so, should one adhere to a doctrine such as Hegel's in his *Phenomenology of the Mind* or to such as Bradley's in his *Appearance and Reality?* Can it be that appearances are in some way gathered up and transmuted in the depth of reality, which contains them at its lowest level, while, at the same time, absorbing, refuting and transcending them? Are we not deceived by words in asserting that such an integration is possible? Naturally, I was sharply aware of the problem of fault, error and pain. Was not Bradley, when he spoke of transmutation, concerned exclusively with contents of thought which are indeed capable of readjustment, like the muddled pieces of a jigsaw which can be assembled correctly? But was there not, precisely, something in the nature of an error or a fault which is not an element of content at all? I am persuaded that, in all this attempted critique of a philosophy which both attracted me and filled me with suspicion, I was impelled by that same sense of the concrete and that awareness of irreconcilable differences which lay at the origin of my need to create. This and no other was the nodal point of the two forms of development which I was to follow in my work.

Yet this picture would be incomplete if I did not try to bring out the religious background of my philosophical inquiry. Although I dislike going into biographical details on this subject, I can not avoid saying a few words about the religious atmosphere of my home.

My father, who had been brought up as a Catholic, had ceased practising his religion at an early age; imbued with the ideas of Taine, Spencer and Renan, his position was that of the late nineteenth-century agnostics; acutely and gratefully aware of all that which art owes to Catholicism, he regarded Catholic thought itself as obsolete and tainted with absurd superstitions. A free mind, according to him, could not but turn away from such childish beliefs; and I suspect, too, that a kind of basic French paganism rebelled in him against the subjection of human nature to Catholic asceticism. Not that he was in the least a hedonist or a traditional Epicurean: few people, I think, have had a stricter or more disciplined life or a more developed sense of their duties of state.

My aunt, who brought me up, and to whose admirable example I owe that need of rigorous truth to which I have tried to do justice in my writings, was of a very different cast of mind. Of Jewish stock, but coming of a family which was wholly indifferent to religion, she was converted to Protestantism, yet showed by her choice of a pastor that her reason rejected its dogmatic beliefs and that she could accept it only in its most liberal form. Imbued with the pessimism of the nineteenth-century poets from Vigny to Mme. Ackermann, she had an acute and implacable sense of the absurdity of existence. Nature, if not utterly evil, at least indifferent to right and wrong, was to her completely unreliable. In the essentially uninhabitable world in which an incomprehensible play of circumstances had caused us to be born, there was only one resource: to forget oneself, to strive to lighten the burden of one's fellow sufferers, and to submit to the most severe self-discipline, for outside this there was nothing but licence.

The truth is that the same invincible agnosticism was common to the outlook of my father and of my aunt, though they gave it different expressions: the one æsthetic, the other ethical; it created around me an unstable and arid climate in which, as I now realise, I found it difficult to breathe. I was not, however, conscious of this at the time, nor did I envy those of my friends who received a religious upbringing. It is true that not many of them did; but I never troubled to find out what spiritual benefit those few of my school-mates who came from religious institutions had derived from their education. I suspected that it was nil; I vaguely thought that it was only just possible for intelligent people in our era to be Protestants, because Protestantism implied private judgment, but that no one could remain a Catholic without a great deal of silliness and hypocrisy. Thus I cannot say that I missed consciously as a child the religious training which I was not given. What is true, however, is that, in spite of the tender care of my aunt and of my maternal grandmother, who was one of the kindest and most generous people I have ever known, I was racked by a kind of tension which at times reached an almost intolerable degree. Consciously, I suffered from the exaggerated attention devoted to me as an only child. My illnesses, my successes and failures at school were given an absurd importance. I felt watched, spied upon; I guessed that, after I had gone to bed, the conversation in the drawing-room turned on my inadequacies and on what could be expected of me. Our school system, if it is not to do positive harm, should be balanced by a goodly dose of scepticism and indifference on the part of the family, but in my case there was no such corrective. My parents had been brilliant pupils and they gave too much importance to my marks and to my places in class. Thus, every composition became a drama. I felt each time that it was a test of my whole being, since no distinction seemed to be made between my scholastic output and myself.

Naturally, I express these things now in a language which I could not have used then; but I am quite sure that this anxiety is at the root of the hateful memories I have kept of my school days, and that it also colours my judgment of our scholastic system which, I still think, totally ignores the facts and particularly the modes of human growth. Thus I am convinced that although I was "an excellent pupil" and won every prize from the bottom class to the top, my intellectual development in fact suffered a set-back throughout the whole of that time, while my health has never wholly recovered from the effect of those years.

All this is less irrelevant to the question of religion than

may appear at first sight. My education roused in me an obscure revolt, not, indeed, against my family, of whom I was
passionately fond, but against what we should now call the
system of values ultimately bound up with the desert universe in which I was expected to live. I can still feel the
exasperation provoked in me by the image of the little livid
archetype of all perfect pupils who sat in my class and with
whom I was continually compared. The thought of this
measuring rod, of this incessant evaluation, put me beside
myself with rage, and it accounts for many a stormy scene
which I remember only vaguely, but which left me broken
rather than repentant.

The words "desert universe" may occasion surprise. But
it must be remembered that my whole childhood and probably my whole life have been overshadowed by the death of
my mother, a death which was completely sudden and
which shook the existence of all of us. Judging from what
I have heard of her and from her letters, full of sparkling
vivacity, she was an exceptional person, marvellously ad-
justed to life. My father found in her a matchless companion who shared wholeheartedly in all his tastes and
pursuits. I have few visual memories of her; but she has remained present and mysteriously with me throughout my life.

Nevertheless, it was inevitable that my aunt, who was
perhaps equally gifted but very different from her in character, should have overshadowed her in fact. So that there
was a strange duality in my life between a being who had
vanished—of whom, whether through shyness or discretion
we hardly ever spoke, and about whom, through a kind of
reverential awe, I could not ask questions—and another—
dominating, self-assertive and convinced that it was her
duty to shed light into the inmost crevices of my mind. I

believe now that this disparity, this hidden polarity between the seen and the unseen, has played a far greater part in my life and thought than any other influence which may be apparent in my writings.

It is clear to me now, as I look back on the difficult years which preceded my initiation to philosophy, that my incessant anxiety was coloured by an obscure sense of the irrevocable and of death. I can explain in no other way the terror which gripped me at night whenever my parents stayed out late at a dinner party or a theatre.

When I was eight, my father held for a short time the post of Minister Plenipotentiary at Stockholm; the Swedish landscape of trees, water and rocks, of which I was to keep a nostalgic memory, symbolised for me, I think, my own sorrowful inward world. During the whole of that year I was allowed to stay away from school, and I found a certain pleasure in getting to know other children from the diplomatic corps and at guessing at their attractively strange background. Thus I combined the enjoyment of being at home and of coming into touch with a varied and exotic world to which I was spontaneously drawn by my taste for travel and for foreign countries.

The *lycée* to which I was sent eighteen months after our return from Sweden struck me as a painful contrast to that free, personal life with its vista open on to the unknown. I think my aversion to it must have been at the root of my growing horror of the spirit of abstraction, of which the school was a kind of absurd palladium. What, indeed, could have been more abstract than our relationship with our masters or even with one another, not to speak of the notions which were inculcated in our minds? There was hardly anything in all this that could touch our sensibility or fulfil our most pressing inward needs. For my own part, if my taste for letters was not destroyed in spite of the encouragement of my father's prodigious culture, it was no thanks to the school, which disgusted me for years with almost every one of the writers whom we studied in class.

All this may seem both irrelevant and indiscrete. But really, it is only at the intersection of all these lines that I can hope to trace the development of which my first writings marked the stages.

The exasperation which was roused in me by our abstract and inhuman school system, is inseparable in my mind from my deeper if less conscious revolt against the world in which I was expected to live, a world hedged with moral restrictions and ravaged by despair. It was a world subject to the strangest condominium of morality and of death. Yet in writing all this I am shocked by my unfairness to those who surrounded my childhood with so tender and so constant a solicitude, and who could not possibly suspect the anxiety and the tension to which they subjected me. This proves to me once again that, at bottom, to think, to formulate and to judge is always to betray.

The holidays were to me each time an oasis in my waste land. Every year we went away to the mountains, always to some different place. My grandmother and my aunt were prevailed upon in their kindness to give in to my tastes and even to my fancies. I remember a long and difficult journey to Hohenschwangau in the Bavarian Alps undertaken at my insistence; and there were many other such occasions. . . . My greatest joy in my childhood was to discover, to explore, to imagine more than I could see, to plan other journeys, complementary and more distant. . . . The hours I have spent dreaming over place-names! And how great was my

delight when I read later in Proust his description of the
kind of crystallisation of feeling around a name charged
with imaginary sensations. My predilection for the inacces-
sible and the unknown went with a disdain, which shocks
me to-day, for whatever is within the reach of all. There
was a lot of vanity in all this, a lot of snobbery, but there
was also something else: a childish horror of what has lost
its freshness, the ingenuous and absurd notion that what is
distant in space is also the untrodden, the undefiled, is that
with which the soul contracts an enchanting intimacy,
whereas the familiar and the nearby has been distorted and
polluted by the stale gushing of Sunday trippers. It was, of
course, an absurd optical delusion, for Hohenschwangau
represented to the Munich shopkeeper just what Chambord
meant to the tripper from Paris. All the same, I think that
I am right in seeing in this predilection something of the
metaphysical concern to discover the intimate at the heart
of the remote, a concern, that is to say, not to overcome
distance by speed, but to wrest from it the spiritual secret
which destroys its power as a barrier. I think I have never
felt attracted to speed for its own sake; what mattered to me
was to discover an *elsewhere* which should be essentially a
here. The world seemed to me then, as now, an indeterminate place in which to extend as much as possible the
region where one is at home and to decrease that which is
vaguely imagined or known only by hearsay, in an abstract
and lifeless manner. I think that my love of travel has always been bound up with the need to make the world inward to me by becoming, as it were, a naturalised citizen of
the greater part of it. For a long time I was influenced by
the idea that in my own country this naturalisation had
been achieved once and for all, but that in others it re-

mained to be conquered. Perhaps that is why I was so impressed by strangeness and surrounded the remoter parts of our continent with a kind of magic halo; oddly enough, the completely exotic countries attracted me less, no doubt because I had no hope to take root in them, to discover in them a new home which, at the same time, should be truly mine. That is why I would suggest that the metaphysics of *at home* of which I have traced the outlines in my *Du Refus à l'Invocation* already underlay my apparently childish fancies. It took me years to understand that my passionate longing for the unknown had nothing to do with a tourist's conscientious inspection of places of note, which convention forced me to carry out, and that the relationship I desired to establish with the countries I explored could not be achieved in this way. The categories I strove to establish later, particularly in *Etre et Avoir*, give meaning to these distinctions and bring out their philosophical basis; but if I felt the need to establish them, it was because I needed to understand and to give shape to my own immediate experience.

It was this experience of discovery which, perhaps more than anything else, awoke in me the desire for the concrete, the nature of which I strove later to understand. (Another aspect of this experience came to me at an early age through deciphering music.) Thinking about it now, I find it odd that, for such a long time, the whole of this holiday world remained apart from my philosophic activity, like a kind of reservation in which I allowed experience to proliferate without submitting it to the control of thought. But perhaps it was a lucky dispensation of the Powers that watch over our growth: no doubt I needed to have in my life this kind of enclosure outside the glare of concentrated attention which, if it is liberating, is also costly in anxiety and in effort. It was as if in the course of my travels and even of my walks, whenever a walk turned into a voyage of discovery, I found myself happily free of that need to make out, to understand or to invent, which conferred upon my life its weight and its interest but also its mortification.

Such are, I think, the main elements I have to keep in mind to answer the question how far my preoccupations were religious at the time of my adolescence. I can hardly doubt, for instance, that the emotion I experienced at the sight of certain Swedish or Italian landscapes was religious in its essence. Not that this emotion ever led me to adopt the metaphysics of pantheism. For some reason, pantheism never attracted me—perhaps because it seemed to me to leave no room for the concrete fullness of personal life.

Perhaps I have said enough to explain which of the problems of philosophy were to assume for me a tormenting sharpness, and which appeared to me, on the contrary, as of merely academic interest. Among these last was the problem of the reality of the outward world, as it is stated in philosophical text-books. None of the extremist forms of Idealism which deny this reality ever seemed to me convincing: for to what more certain or more intimate experience could this reality be opposed? The real question seemed to me to find out of what kind was the existence which Idealism vainly attempted to deny, and whether, in the last analysis, it did not vastly exceed its outward appearances. From this angle at least I might well have been attracted to Schopenhauer, had I not distrusted the rudimentary ontology which underlies his critique of knowledge, and had I not been unwilling to subscribe to a thesis which is so fatal to individuality both in ourselves and in those we love. I think I have always been repelled by doctrines which evade difficulties or invent a special terminology to cover them up as if they were a bad taste or a bad smell. Thus I rebelled very early on against the way in which Idealism overrates the part of construction in sensual perception, to the point of pushing aside to the confines of non-being all such concrete and unforeseeable detail as not only clothes experience, but gives it its flavour of reality. I suspect that my grievance against transcendental idealism stimulated my inquiry into the metaphysical implications of sense-experience as such, and that my general tendency to bring out difficulties instead of concealing them helped to develop my distrust of systems of philosophy of whatever kind: for there is no system that does not involve the temptation to declare *a priori* that this or that difficulty is to be judged unimportant and consequently set aside. I believe now more than ever that it is the first duty of a philosopher to resist this temptation, which seems somehow to form part of his very calling.

At the beginning, however, my reaction against Idealism developed inside a framework of thought which was itself Idealist, or which, at any rate, still owed a good deal to Idealist categories. This accounts for much of what is difficult, irritating and even repellent in the first part of my *Journal Métaphysique*. I was like a man who is irked by a suit of clothes which is too tight for him, and which he is vainly trying to discard. What strikes me as particularly strange about my reactions at that time is the partiality they show for beliefs which, in all good faith, I could not have said that I held. Strictly speaking, all I did was to try to discern the transcendental conditions of faith, held in all its purity, without committing myself in any way or prejudging, at least in principle, the metaphysical value or the reality of such faith. It does not seem to me, however, that this distinction could be seriously upheld, and it was in fact precluded by the nature of my inquiry which assumed that faith could not be regarded as a hypothesis, and sought to establish the existence of an unverifiable truth transcending the progress of knowledge within the particular fields of science. Under the circumstances, it became impossible for me to maintain on the purely religious level the attitude which is still mine on the metapsychical plane and which consists in saying: granted that this or that fact has been proved experimentally, how can we account for it? Is it necessary, in order to assign to it its proper place, to revise or even to reverse this or that postulate which has been admitted without discussion? On the metapsychical plane experience is the decisive factor; it remains to be established that telepathy is a fact or that premonitions are real. But it would have seemed to me, on the face of it, scandalous to subject religious faith conceived in its purity to such an empirical test. Faith seemed to me by its essence beyond all possible experimental confirmation or disproof. There remained the question, which I was not then in a position to tackle, as to what is meant by the term "purity." What, in fact, was the religious essence which I was attempting to grasp? Doubtless I was trying to separate this essence from what I would have called the impurities which are the target of all forms of sociological analysis. But in this, did I not share the illusion of those who hope to establish, beyond all confessional differences, a religion founded on reason to which every man of good faith must—or should be able to—subscribe? I can assert that I was never taken in by this fiction. I quite clearly remember denouncing as far

back as 1912 what I described as "religious Esperantism";
this was inevitable from the moment when I recognised that
the subject of faith cannot be treated as a modality of
thought in general and that, in consequence, there can be
no *glauben überhaupt*; in other words, that belief is the
attitude of a subject who is individual and concrete, but
who, nevertheless, must not be confused with the empirical
I, for the simple reason that this *I* can be reduced to a whole
which is made up of objectively definable determinations.
This assertion, which it is so difficult to paraphrase in concrete terms, still seems to me to sum up all I have ever
thought on this subject; I can honestly say that I arrived at
it by myself, for it was before I had read Kierkegaard, in
whom I might so easily have found it.

During the last three years before the war of 1914, I
pursued, outside the beaten track, the inquiries that were to
lead me to my first existentialist statements. It is difficult
to-day to recall the atmosphere of that time: it is so remote
from ours that it is hard to imagine it. It is not that we did
not think about war, or that we did not have premonitions:
I have a particularly poignant memory of the Agadir alarm.
But we tried hard to believe that humanity in the West
could withstand the assault of the forces that were driving
it towards catastrophe. I think that not one of us could
suspect the fragility, the precariousness, of the civilisation
which enveloped us like a tegument; a civilisation on which
the wealth of centuries seemed to have conferred a solidity
we would have thought it madness to question. For my
part, I cannot think without nostalgia of the dusk of that
Europe in which the material conditions of life seemed to
be so easy, and where communication between countries
was almost untrammelled. We ought no doubt to have

guessed that this euphoria was a snare and that this facility concealed the worst dangers; but I do not remember that we ever suspected it. For my part, the illusion in which we lived enabled me to conclude the preliminary but also the most difficult part of my work. The shock administered by the war explains the change of tone and of key which is noticeable in the second part of my *Journal*. I should perhaps say a few words about the circumstances in which I found myself. Precluded from active service by the poor state of my health, I was asked by Xavier Léon in August, 1914, to take his place at the head of the Information Service organised by the Red Cross. Our work consisted at first in obtaining news of the wounded who were hospitalised in the ambulances of the *Union des Femmes de France*; it turned out, however, that these were nearly always able to write to their families, and we were soon besieged with inquiries about others of whom nothing had been heard. Thanks to the reports on the wounded and the prisoners which we had at our disposal, we were often able to get into touch with the comrades or the officers of the missing men; needless to say, in the great majority of cases what we had to report was the news of their death. Every day I received personal visits from the unfortunate relatives who implored us to obtain what information we could; so that in the end every index card was to me a heart-rending personal appeal. Nothing, I think, could have immunised me better against the power of effacement possessed by the abstract terms which fill the reports of journalists and historians of the war.

One effect of the inquiries which I undertook was to make me reflect upon the limitations of any inquiry or questionnaire, so that I began to ask myself if it was not possible to get beyond the sphere in which the mind proceeds by way of question and answer. At this point I must refer to the part played in my development by the metapsychical experiments which I carried out in the winter of 1916–17 and of which I spoke a few months later to Henri Bergson. The result of these experiments made it impossible for me to doubt the reality of metapsychical phenomena; I must insist on this all the more because I have not mentioned it in any of my writings since my *Journal Métaphysique,* and it might be thought that on my conversion to Catholicism I repudiated this conviction. This would not be true. I am as persuaded as ever that the philosopher must take metapsychical facts into consideration, and that he cannot assimilate these facts unless he discards certain speculative prejudices; one of the advantages of such an inquiry is precisely that it makes him conscious of such postulates, which are often implicit in his mind. There is no domain in which it would be more valuable to continue Bergson's research; he has been the only French thinker who has recognised the importance of metapsychical data, and the thesis which he has put forward so strongly in *L'Energie Spirituelle* is in no way annulled by *Les Deux Sources de la Morale et de la Religion.* At the same time, I persist in thinking that the demarcation line between the normal and the abnormal is, to say the least, uncertain; it is enough to consider the normal in the strange light shed by a sufficiently advanced meditation for it to appear supra-normal. As I have said elsewhere, the pseudo-idea of the "altogether natural" has contributed not only to discolour our universe, but also to decentralise it and to empty it of those principles which conferred upon it meaning and life. If metapsychical research can assist us to turn back from this disastrous path, this is enough to make it worthy of the attention of the philosopher. Far be it from me to deny that the explorer in this domain often feels bogged or up against a blank wall. For reasons which are as yet unknown but which could doubtless be discovered if the human mind brought to bear upon this subject the sustained effort of analysis it has displayed elsewhere, we meet here with a dimension of the human or the supra-human world which does not lend itself to the indefinite progression of knowledge such as has taken place in the field of natural science. All the evidence goes to suggest that we come up against obstacles which are inherent in our condition as men, and that we cannot overcome these obstacles without an interior transformation which we cannot operate by ourselves. The only genuine inward mutation of which experience offers us irrefutable proof takes place in the order of mysticism and is therefore inconceivable without the hidden impulse of grace. Metapsychical research exposes its devotee to the temptation of thinking that he can, either by his own means or through the assistance of forces which he hopes to control, accede to a mode of power unknown to positive science; to this extent the distrust felt by spiritual people is justified. There is no doubt that this expectation is not simply an illusion; the belief that it is proceeds from an almost idolatrous faith in science and technics. It remains true, nevertheless, that along this hazardous way an intoxicating sense of certainty is often followed abruptly by complete discouragement; no doubt a balance is struck in the end, but it does not go without a deep and humble realisation of our own weakness and of the darkness which envelopes us almost completely. I say almost, because, at curiously irregular intervals, it is lit up in flashes, and this, given certain precautions, may perhaps justify the philosopher in calling upon the seer. Not that any formal alliance is conceivable between the two, but only a kind of tacit understanding which is strengthened or weakened in accordance with events. Admittedly, nothing is less satisfactory from the rational point of view than a relationship so secret, so precarious and which is at times so near to complicity. But then should not the notion of the satisfactory itself be subjected to a rigorous critique? Whatever its ultimate meaning, the universe into which we have been thrown cannot satisfy our reason, let us have the courage to admit it once and for all. To deny it is not only scandalous, but in some ways truly sinful; and indeed I am convinced that this is precisely the besetting sin of the philosopher, the sin of Leibnitz and, less obviously, the sin of Hegel. The supreme mission of the philosopher cannot consist in proclaiming a certain number of official truths liable to rally votes at international congresses. In the last analysis, such truths inevitably turn out to be sheer platitudes. The imperishable glory of a Kierkegaard or a Nietzsche consists perhaps mainly in this, that they have proved, not only by their arguments, but by their trials and by their whole life, that a philosopher worthy of the name cannot be a man of congresses, and that he deviates from his path every time that he allows himself to be torn from the solitude which is his calling. It is only by clinging to this solitude that he remains at the disposal of those who await from him, if not a lead, at least a stimulation. Here again the satisfactory must be put aside; after all it is no more than a scholastic category. A candidate's answer to an examiner is or is not satisfactory; but then in an examination there are clearly formulated rules and the stage has been set in advance, whereas in the real world, which is, or should be, that of the philosopher, there is nothing of the kind. The stage always remains to be set; in a sense everything always starts from zero, and a philosopher is not worthy of the name unless he not only accepts but wills this harsh necessity. Whereas the temptation for a congress man is always to refer to an earlier congress where it was stablished that . . . This perpetual beginning again, which may seem scandalous to the scientist or the technician, is an inevitable part of all genuinely philosophical work; and perhaps it reflects in its own order the fresh start of every new awakening and of every birth. Does not the very structure of duration and of life show that philosophical thought is unfaithful to reality whenever it attempts to proceed from conclusion to conclusion towards a *Summa* which, in the end, needs only to be expounded and memorised paragraph by paragraph? The conviction that reality cannot be "summed up," that this is indeed the last way in which it can be apprehended, came to me very early, partly as a result of reading Bradley. It seemed to me from then on that there was a danger of making an illicit use of the idea of integration, and that the more one relied on the richest and most concrete data of experience, the less this idea appeared to be applicable to reality. From this point of view, I think I can now say that, without ever regarding pluralism as a tenable metaphysical doctrine, I have always been inclined to believe that it had, at least, a negative value—the value of a refusal, of a necessary protest; though my own tendency has been rather to deny the ontological importance which metaphysicians, from the school of Aelia to the time of Hegel, have assigned to the opposition between the one and the many.

What started me on the way to denying the idea of an

intelligible whole which is at the same time the motive principle and the end of dialectics, was, I think, primarily the consideration of action as something other than a mere content of thought. Is it that I was particularly receptive to the idea of action as a break, to what we would now call its revolutionary character? I would say rather—although this is only a *nuance*—that I have always been struck by its originality, or even by the singularity of the perspective by which it is inevitably governed. This is why I was attracted by monadism; and I might even have adopted this doctrine for good if the thesis of the incommunicability of monads had not seemed to me a challenge to experience and to common sense, while the notion of a pre-established harmony struck me as a pure invention as ingenious as it was artificial. To act was, to my mind, primarily equivalent to taking up a position, and it was only by a pure fiction that reality could be made to integrate the act whereby I took up my position in regard to it. Looking back on it now, I see that I was trying to establish a concrete and dramatic type of relationship in place of the abstract relationships of inherence or of exteriority between which traditional philosophies claimed to make me choose.

Strange as it may seem, I do not think that my concern with maintaining the primacy of action has ever expressed itself, as it has with others, in a philosophy of liberty. The traditional problem of liberty has never worried me to any great extent: I have always held that man could not but have the liberty which he required, and that, consequently, there was no real problem. So that this was never the centre of my philosophical anxiety. Granted the traditional distinction between philosophies of being and philosophies of liberty, I would say that my spontaneous tendency was towards the former. Not that I was conscious of it; indeed, in so far as I still followed in the footsteps of the criticists and even of Bergson, I was inclined to regard philosophies of being as philosophies of *das Ding* and to mistrust them accordingly. My effort can be best described as an attempt to establish a concept which precludes all equation of being with *Ding* while upholding the ontological without going back to the category of substance which I regarded with profound mistrust. It was in the light of this major pre-occupation that I reflected upon faith and later upon fidelity; in particular, I think that the expression in *Etre et Avoir*, "being as the place of fidelity," gives the clue to my previous inquiries and at the same time heralds a new stage. The same could be said of many expressions in *Homo Viator* and especially in *Phénoménologie de l'Espérance*. Perhaps I can best explain my continual and central metaphysical preoccupation by saying that my aim was to discover how a subject, in his actual capacity as subject, is related to a reality which cannot in this context be regarded as objective, yet which is persistently required and recognised as real. Such inquiries could not be carried out without going beyond the kind of psychology which limits itself to defining attitudes without taking their bearing and concrete intention into account. This is what accounts for the convergence of the metaphysical and the religious which became apparent in my earliest writings. Perhaps I should again note the manner in which this convergence was justified from the point of view which I held as far back as my first *Journal*. What this point of view tended ultimately to exclude was the idea that the mind can, as it were, objectively define the structure of reality and then regard itself as qualified to legislate for it. My own idea was, on the contrary, that the undertaking had to be pursued within reality itself, to which the philosopher can never stand in the relationship of an onlooker to a picture. Thus my inquiry anticipated the conception of mystery as I later defined it in my paper, *On the Ontological Mystery*. This leads me to believe that the development of my thought was largely an explicitation. It all seems to me to have happened as though I only gradually succeeded in treating as material for thought what had been an immediate experience, an experience less realised than assumed, rather like the blind groping in an unchartered cave; it is only later that the prospector can understand and retrace the way travelled in this first period of discovery. Moreover, I am convinced that I can be creative as a philosopher only for so long as my experience still contains unexploited and unchartered zones. And this explains at last what I said earlier on about experience being like a promised land: it has to become, as it were, its own beyond, inasmuch as it has to transmute itself and make its own conquest. After all, the error of empiricism consists only in ignoring the part of invention and even of creative initiative involved in any genuine experience. It might also be said that its error is to take experience for granted and to ignore its mystery; whereas what is amazing and miraculous is that there should be experience at all. Does not the deepening of metaphysical knowledge consist essentially in the steps whereby experience, instead of evolving technics, turns inwards towards the realisation of itself?